Business Case Studies

Prof Javed Iqbal Saani, PhD

Intellectual Capital Enterprise

CONTENTS

PREFACE   XI

LIST OF EXIBITS   XV

INTRODUCTION TO CASE STUDIES   1

1 CHEETHAM MEAT & POULTRY (CPM)   5

2 PROJECT MANAGEMENT IN ABACUS BROWSERS LIMITED (ABL)   25

3 SOFTWARE DEVELOPMENT IN EAGLES (SDE)   55

4 PTCL AND PRIVATISATION OF TELECOM INDUSTRY   71

5 LASANI & COMPANY (PVT) LTD   93

6 NORTHERN CEMENT LTD (NCL)   97

7 PTCL AND COMPETITIVE EDGE   101

8 INFORMATION BASED DECISIONS   105

9 CENTRAL ASIAN AIRWAYS CORPORATION (CAAC)   111

10 INFORMATION SYSTEM AT TAXILA HERITAGE   115

11 PROFESSIONAL BOOK PUBLISHING BUSINESS   119

12 NORTHERN ROCKS (NR), PAKISTAN LIMITED   125

13 HARIPURE TELECOM (HT)   129

14 E-COMMERCE IN VIRTUAL BUSINESS (VB)   133

15 KNOWLEDGE MANAGEMENT IN TAASCO   137

BIBLIOGRAPHY   143

INDEX   165

ABOUT THE AUTHOR   171

OTHER BOOKS BY THE AUTHOR (S)   173

Abu'd-Darda' (RA) said, "I heard the Messenger of Allah, may Allah bless him and grant him peace, say,

1. 'Allah will make the path to the Garden easy for anyone who travels a path in search of knowledge.
2. Angels spread their wings for the seeker of knowledge out of pleasure for what he is doing.
3. Everyone in the heavens and everyone in the earth ask forgiveness for a man of knowledge, even the fish in the water.
4. The superiority of the man of knowledge to the man of worship is like the superiority of the moon to all the planets.
5. The men of knowledge are the heirs of the Prophets.
6. The Prophets bequeath neither dinar nor dirham; they bequeath knowledge. Whoever takes it has taken an ample portion.'"

[Abu Dawud and at-Tirmidhi; Riyadh us Salihin, Hadith 1388, p. 211]

Dedication

To the entire Ummah who has embraced the message of prophet (ﷺ) and is sacrificing because they proclaim that Allah is their Rubb, Quran is their book and Muhammad (ﷺ) is their leader.

Acknowledgement

My gratitude is due to my family who spared me to embark on the project. They also provide valuable information which enriched the contents of this effort. May Allah reward them for their contribution? Ameen! My thanks is also due to the companies who allow me to write about them.

x

PREFACE

Teaching through case studies is an integral part of contemporary curriculum strategy. The concepts, theories and techniques described in books are abstract in nature. Social sciences like management / business administration reflect the human behaviour at work in principal associated with research in the area. The case studies augment them with real life exemplars in pragmatic situations. Therefore, theory is put in practice or theory is shown in practical situations. It helps to understand underpinned phenomenon easily. It also helps the learners to conceptualise the reality of pros and cons of management. And enhances the usefulness of management as a discipline.

Most of the cases in the volume were written at different occasions. For instance, the first case emerged when I wrote the first book on project management i.e. Understanding Project Management. Another was added when I wrote "Managing Risk in Projects". One of my M. Phil student was from PTCL. It helped me to access the organisation and I have conducted the case study. I have added the "Lasani Case" while I was teaching a module in Iqra University, Islamabad Campus. Remaining short cases were written when I wrote "Understanding Information Systems". Later on, the Higher Education Commission (HEC) of Pakistan recognised the book as a piece of research equivalent to X category work.

The focus of the first three cases is project management including the one about managing risk. They are semi-solved but the case questions try to explore issues raised during the course of design or implementation of a given solution. The next one deals with the management of change. The fifth one is concerned with looming profitability. The goal of the rest of the cases is management information systems (MIS). Consequently, e-commerce and knowledge management are talked about. Some are discussing generic business issues. Thus, a range of subjects makes the collection useful for a variety of audience.

The bibliography is added for the researchers to access relevant sources; the author has taken benefit of the sources compiled.

The authors welcome comments and suggestions from academia and practitioners for further improvements in the future.

Prof Javed Iqbal Saani, PhD

9 December 2017, Manchester

1 Cheetham Meat & Poultry (CPM)

Exhibit 1 Details of the project

Exhibit 2 Specialism of staff members

Exhibit 3 The milestones

Exhibit 4 Bar chart of milestones

Exhibit 5 Responsibility chart according to milestones

Exhibit 6 Responsibility chart of milestones

Exhibit 7 Responsibilities chart for M2

Exhibit 8 Responsibilities chart for M3

Exhibit 9 Responsibility chart of milestones

Exhibit 10 The progress report day one

Exhibit 11 Product wise analysis of project

Exhibit 12 Allocation of workload

Exhibit 13 Activities and their duration

Exhibit 14 Assumptions of men-hours

calculation

2 Project Management in Abacus Browsers Limited (ABL)

Exhibit 1 Specification of the proposed website

Exhibit 2 Requirements of the project

Exhibit 3 The components of the website

Exhibit 4   Millstone template

Exbibit 5 Milestones

Exhibit 6 Project organization

Exhibit 7 Organization of SHARP

Exhibit 8 Responsibility chart of various milestones

Exhibit 9 Activity chart for design

Exhibit 10 Millstone and their details

Exhibit 11 Phase bar chart

Exhibit 12 Progress report of week 1 of design team

Exhibit 13 The balance of work remaining at the end of the first week (the second week of the project)

Exhibit 14 The amount of work completed

Exhibit 15 The   balance   of   work (Percentage)

Exhibit 16 Project risk management strategy in ABL

3 Software Development in Eagles (SDE)

Exhibit 1 The Requirement of SPL project

Exhibit 2 Duration of Activities (in men-hours)

Exhibit 3 Allocation of activities to team members

Exhibit 4 Sequence and dependencies of activities

Exhibit 5 Network diagram of activities

Exhibit 6 Duration of activities on the network

Exhibit 7 Calculation of critical path

Exhibit 8 Determination of Cost

Exhibit 9 Weekly progress report of Mr. Jones

Exhibit 10 Progress report of activities

4 PTCL and privatisation of Telecom Industry

Exhibit 1 Evolution of PTCL

Exhibit 2 Brief history of PTCL

5 Information Based Decisions

Exhibit 1 National production, usage by Refaan and price over last seven years

6 Knowledge Management in TAASCO

Exhibit 1 Components of a spreadsheet

INTRODUCTION TO CASE STUDIES

Case study is a business story that describes the stages of a project over its life cycle. Case-based analysis begun in law and medical science. The decision made by jurists became an exemplar for the other lawyers and judges to form their opinion about a certain case. The medical professionals also adopt the same for treatment of patients. It is a recent phenomenon in management sciences; project management has no exception. Case study is also a research approach based on qualitative paradigm. It is widely used for teaching purpose in business schools these days. It is because a business situation is described in a teaching case with plethora of data. The job of learners is to analyse it to gain understanding and identify alternatives in order to arrive a given solution.

Case study is bombarded with data. It may include history of the organization, its products and services, organization structure, customer base, financial management tools, revenue stream; its relations with partners, competitors and other parties in the country or market. Problems encountered and solutions adopted to resolve the issues.

The analysis strategy is generic rather than a specific. Our case studies are partially solved. Here a problem or opportunity arises as a result of an order placed by a customer. The organization forms a team to fulfil it. The team undergoes the project management process. Project initiation, planning, resources allocation and implementation/monitoring and control. One of the case also discusses the risk associated with the project.

The team has adopted one of the many ways available to resolve the issue. Teachers and learners can identify other alternatives to find out other viable solutions. The purpose of the case is not to find out an optimum solution but to follow a process of encountering problems and the strategy to address it. It provides a learning opportunity to apply it in similar situations in practice.

There are many kinds of cases in management perspective. Some researchers write articles about case of various entities: organisations, people or products. Master or doctorate level researchers also conduct case studies as part of their research projects. Many of them publish their work later on. Text book writers also include cases for illustrative purpose. The present collection falls under the category. The purpose is to elaborate the subject contents with the help of case studies. It provides an opportunity to the students to understand the concepts and apply them in real life situations.

Yin (2003) has worked extensively about the nature and functions of case studies. His work is concerned with how to conduct and compile case studies in business organisations and elsewhere.

1 CHEETHAM MEAT & POULTRY (CPM)

Introduction

The principles of PM are applicable in any organization irrespective of its size, nature of business or mode of organization (sole proprietor, partnership, public limited). It is the common view that project management is applicable in large projects, in bigger organizations. A few studies address applications of project management concepts in retail industry. This case study examines it in retail perspective. There are numerous industries that implicitly or explicitly apply project management principles; the authors have chosen meat retailers to examine the phenomenon. It is a mini case study on a mini entity.

Cheetham meat and poultry (CMP) was established in 2005 to serve the local community with a view to capture lion share of the market. Most of other meat shops were not functioning as an independent concern they work as a part of a cash and carry or a retail outlet. However, CMP deals with meat and poultry products only. CMP is located in the heart of Cheetham village; it has a huge storage facility (cold store) where they can hang 40 lambs at a time. CMP has a 10 feet long display refrigerator and cutting

Exhibit 1	Details of the project			
Item	Name	Quantity	Packing size	Delivery date
1	Mutton	300kg	3kg	10.5.2017
2	Chaps	200kg	1kg	"
3	Mince	100kg	1kg	"
4	Chicken	500kg	1kg	"
5	Boneless meat	200kg	2kg	"
6	Drum stick	200kg or 800 pieces	2kg (10 pieces)	"
7	Fish spiced	50kg	2kg	"
8	Fish without spiced	50kg	2	"
9	Chicken mince	200kg	2kg	"

10	Chicken wings	200kg	2kg	"

worktop of the same size, five personnel are working in addition to the owner manager Mr. Shan. CMP owns an electronic cutting machine, a mince machine, lot of knives and another cutlery. Two electronic cash registers are available for customer service. Beef, mutton, fish and whole chicken are principal raw material. The company manufactures 15 products including simple mutton, beef, ribs, mince, and spare parts of animals. Chicken product includes boneless thy, boneless chest, wings legs, whole chicken, baby chicken, spare parts such as hearts and stomach are the key chicken products. (Exhibit 1)

Fish products are relatively limited: whole fish, marinated fish and spiced fish are available. Although financial results are not available yet; the management was satisfied with the performance and perceives it a successful business.

The company has not expended much in the last five years, except hiring of two personnel to meet the increased demand; customer waiting time during peak hours is 15 to 20

minutes; the business customer usually receive their deliveries on time because they place their orders in advance.

The company received an order of 2000 kg of mixed products of mutton, chicken, and fish. Table 1shows the details of the project/ order for analysis of the case study.

Project planning at CMP

Purpose of planning, according to Anderson and his colleague are to gain common understanding, obtaining overview of the work to be completed. It lays down the foundation for resource allocation and forming appropriate organization structure for the project that provides guidelines for subsequent work and defining a programme of monitoring and control.

The manager of CMP called a meeting to discuss the project and related issues. The meeting was attended by all the members of the staff since the project was to be completed with daily or normal task (the detail will be discussed later on under the project organization). The manager described the details of the project as mentioned in table1. The project will have to be completed within four weeks in addition to the normal workload; the existing members of the team would carry out it without additional hiring or over time arrangements. The manager believes it is viable because all members of the staff are busy only in peak times usually 1100 to 1600 daily. The shop opens at 0900 and closes at 1800 daily, seven days a week; it provides a 4 hour slake time daily for each employee.

Mr. Shah, the manager estimates that CMP would need 30 lambs for mutton products, 1800 chickens and 100 whole fish to deliver the order. The project was managed by five personnel excluding the manager; it took 100 men hours; 1380 packets were made; each item was packed in hard plastic boxes and each packet was delivered to the customer.

CMP will have men 112 hours available within next four weeks, off which 80% of the time will be required for the project.

The manager, Mr. Shah, informed the staff member about time available and the details of work. Mr. Jan said, "we need to make contingency plan for staff members to cope with uncertainties". Mr. Shah replied he had a plan to hire one or two personnel who will work with us as a fulltime member. In this case, we would have 40 more hours available weekly. We can double this by adding another person in our team; all members agreed with the contingency plan and were hopeful for the project to complete on time.

Although all members of the staff were trained to work on any product or able to cope with any raw material, four persons were specialist for dealing with four types of raw material as shown in the Exhibit 2. The purpose of the table is to ensure that the "right staff" is available at the right place.

Exhibit 2	Specialism of staff members	
Serial No	**Name**	**Animal type**
1	A. Khan	Cows
2	Mr. Bakka	Lambs
3	Arifwala	Chicken
4	Akbar Sindhu	Fish

The next job of the meeting was to allocate the resources. The project uses a range of resources, the worktop, electronic cutting machine, cold store, packing material etc. some of them are shared and others can be used independently; the worktop is big enough to accommodate all personnel at a time. The cutlery is also enough to serve the entire team. However, electronic cutting machine can serve one person at a time. The team members can use it in turn whenever they need it. It saves time without significant loss of productivity. The finished products are stored in a cold store, which has large capacity and is capable to store 8000 kilograms of meat. All the personnel agree to complete the job along with the daily workload. CMP management offers 10% bonus to complete the project for everyone.

As can be seen from the above discussion two teams were formed; one is to cut or manufacture various products and the other to pack them. The first team virtually comprises of all the personnel of organization headed by the manager where he did not do any physical work. The second team consists of four personnel in charge of CMP manager. The details about it will be discussed in the second section of this chapter.

Project activity and milestone planning

Milestones are the key achievements or stages of completion. Anderson and his colleagues view a milestone as "check point in the project, which enables us to ensure that we are on the right track. A milestone is a description of the state the project should be in at certain stages." Milestone should be defined in connection with the solution the project is offering.

Given that, conceptual understanding, CMP defines milestone according to the packing plan described in Exhibit 3 and 4. The largest quantity is chicken-based products followed by mutton and fish. Management has divided the cutting part of the project into three milestones: chicken, mutton and fish, since the former represents 60% of the order followed by mutton 30% and fish 10%. The chicken will be started and finished first; the mutton will be in the middle and fish at the end.

Exhibit 2 depicts the milestones; the length of the bar is according to the percentage of time involved in a milestone. It is noted that there is only one dependency in the milestones; packing needs completion of cutting M1-M3; they had to be completed at one point of time, the M4 can be started than. There is no dependency in the first three milestones, however.

Exhibit 3 The milestones		
	M1 (Chicken)	
Cutting starts	M2 (Mutton)	Packing
	M3 (Fish)	

Exhibit 4 Bar chart of milestones				
	Period 1	Period 2	Period 3	Period 4
M1 Chicken				
M2 Mutton				
M3 Fish				

M4 Packing				

Project organization

Organization refers to, in management literature, the distribution of responsibilities. In terms of project management the division of activities and tasks. Anderson and his colleagues (1995) believe a project is organized or responsibilities are allocated as full time or part time bases. Team members are relieved from all activities or normal jobs to work on a certain project as a full-time member. Alternatively, they can work on the project as a part-time in addition to their daily routine. It is termed as integration of a project to the existing operations.

CMP management decided to choose the second option because the company has to serve daily customer as a mainstream function. If they chose full time option than they have to hire additional staff for the project or some existing members have to be dedicated for the project. This would put additional pressure on them, which jeopardize the equality of work for which the CMP is famous. Secondly, the managers believe that project is manageable with the existing workload and within the required time framework. Other members of the team were also agreed and happy with the arrangement as it does not disturb their daily routine.

The next question for the CMP manager was to choose mode of organization; theoretically, hierarchical and matrix methods are available. Matrix was selected because its merits outweigh its demerits; it is a better option for decision-making and fixes responsibilities, provides better communication, flexible organization, and better use of resource (Anderson et al, 1995). It was important to draw a responsibilities chart to specify key responsibilities for various members of staff which were divided according to the milestones. Exhibit 5-8 demonstrate the responsibilities charts of various staff members individually and collectively.

Exhibit 5 Responsibility chart according to milestones					
Milestone	Staff 1	Staff 2	Staff 3	Staff 4	Staff 5
M1	√	√	√	√	-
M2	-	√	√	√	-
M3	-	-	-	-	√

Exhibit 6 describes the responsibilities chart for milestone 1.

Exhibit 6 Responsibility chart of milestones					
Activity	Staff 1	Staff 2	Staff 3	Staff 4	Staff 5
Whole chicken	√	√	√	√	-
Boneless breast	-	√		-	-
Dram sticks	-	-	√	√	-
Mince	-	-	√	√	-
Chicken wings	√	√	-	-	-

Exhibit 7 describes the responsibilities chart for milestone 2.

Exhibit 7 Responsibilities chart for M2					
Activity	Staff 1	Staff 2	Staff 3	Staff 4	Staff 5
Mutton	√	-	-	-	-
Mince	√	√	-	-	-
Champs	-	-	-	√	-

Exhibit 8 describes the responsibilities chart for milestone 3.

Exhibit 8 Responsibilities chart for M3					
Milestone	Staff 1	Staff 2	Staff 3	Staff 4	Staff 5
Fish spiced	-	-	-	-	√
Fish simple	-	-	-	-	√

The last milestone is packing. Exhibit 9 and 10 shows the responsibilities of the people involved.

Exhibit 9 Responsibility chart of milestones				
Staff	Cow	Lams	Chicken	Fish
1	√			
2			√	√
3		√		
4				√

Project control

Although the project was a medium size venture, yet some controlling mechanism was essential to ensure the project was on track. The pros and cons of it was decided; each member of staff would fill a progress chart daily showing the amount of work he has done out of the project. This chart has to be checked by the manager daily and instruct the relevant member to catch up the work in case someone is behind the schedule.

Project control "involves analysis the situation, deciding what to do and doing it." It is management of project not merely paper works (Anderson et al, 1995). Control requires reporting of progress and taking correct measure, if necessary. A mechanism should be established to ensure timely reporting of progress at milestone level or periodically. Movement of milestone date, changing objectives, injecting additional resources, and rearranges the workload of team members are typical controlling actions (ibid., p.152). Although controlling activities involve the use of resources, time management, schedule adherence, quality control, responsibility chart, changes/additions, waiting time and any special problems in large projects, yet CMP designed a daily progress report, which usually filled by the team members and examined by the manager to ensure progress at milestone levels. Exhibit 10 reflects a progress report for the first day of the project.

The progress report for day 2 starts with balance of the previous day and generates a new balance at the end of the day. The cutting work was completed in three weeks; the final week was reserved for packing. Eight hundred Kilograms were prepared on the second week and the balance was cut in the third week. The packing was done in the fourth week, while the delivery was due in the same week. The project was completed and delivered on time.

Exhibit 10	The progress report day one		
Team member	Total work load (kg)	Completed (kg)	Balance (kg)
Staff 1	450	50	400
Staff 2	450	100	350
Staff 3	450	50	400
Staff 4	450	50	400
Staff 5	200	20	180
Totals	2000	270	1730

Discussion about the case study

The project was a medium size venture for the organization however; most of the project management tools and techniques were applied. Important aspect of project was its completion within time that was the major success criteria for it. Other parameters such as budget and quality were not very important because the products of the project were to be use in marriage function. The client needed it on time; the quality was involved in cleaning the meat from fat and other unnecessary elements. All the personnel were supposed to do that for which they were well trained and experienced, so the quality was not an issue. Budget was also not very significant element because the team members were paid as usual; however, a bonus was paid on the successful completion of the project. Since the project was completed on time, the staff was paid the bonus; the project did not overrun budget.

Milestones were identified and defined prudently based on the competencies of the staff; milestones were allocated to all staff members equally but not to the manager because he used to spend a lion share of time in managerial activities. Consequently, little time remains for operational duties; however, he has done it amicably.

The resources were utilized effectively; the time of each staff member was applied to the best of their capabilities; thus, the project flew in the planned direction over its life cycle. Exhibit 11 and 12 demonstrate the analysis of the project from various perspectives.

Exhibit 11   Product wise analysis of project

Items	Whole chicken	Mince	Boneless breast	Drum sticks	Wings	Simple mutton	Champs	Spiced fish	Simple fish	Total
Chicken	500kg	200kg	200kg	200(80	100					1200
Mutton		100				300	200			600
Fish								100	100	200

Note: The duration of the project was 4 weeks

Each staff cuts 450kg extra except staff 5.

Exhibit 12   Allocation of workload

Items	Staff 1	Staff 2	Staff 3	Staff 4	Staff 5
Chicken	300	300	300	300	
Mutton	150	150	150	150	
Fish					200

Total workload	450	450	450	450	200

The duration of each activity is based upon the assumption that a member of the staff can cut 25kg of any meat on average. Given that Exhibit 13 shows the total men hours required and total men hours available for the project. Also Exhibit 14 shows the assumptions of various calculations.

Exhibit 13 Activities and their duration		
Activity no	**Activity name**	**Activity duration**
1	Whole chicken	20 men hours
2	Chicken mince	8 men hours
3	Boneless breast	8 men hours
4	Drum sticks	8 men hours
5	Wings	4 men hours
6	Mutton mince	4 men hours
7	Simple mutton	12 men hours
8	Champs	8 men hours

9	Fish simple	4 men hours
10	Fish spiced	4 men hours
11	packing	4 men hours
Total		84 men hours

Exhibit 14 Assumptions of men-hours calculation

Assumptions

A staff member can cut 25 kg of any animal in one hour.

Total weight of the project 2000kg

Men hours required for cutting the project=2000/25=80.

Men hours required for packing 20.

Total men hours required for the project=100.

Available men hours during the life of the project=5 (persons) x 8(daily working hours) x 20(number of working days within which the project is to be completed) =160 men hours i.e. 5x8x20 =800 men hours.

Extra time available for daily work=160-100=700 men hours

The above analysis suggests that CMP did more work by applying the principles of project management because daily work was not disturbed and the project was completed as additional work.

Case questions

1. Do you think project management principals have been appropriately applied to CMP?
2. What other PM Principals could be applied to the case study? Provide an example.
3. Has the project management process including planning, organizing and controlling been implemented adequately? If not, what alternatives were available and could be applied for the efficient use of project resources.
4. The management of CMP opted "integration" strategy. Do you agree with the decision? Why and why not?

5. Discuss the suitability of the case study for the subject. What did you learn out of the case study?

2 PROJECT MANAGEMENT IN ABACUS BROWSERS LIMITED (ABL)

ABL was established in early nineties to offer Software Development as a limited company. In 1996 with the advent of the internet the operation was expanded to web development, web hosting and maintenance; training to clients and organizations. The number of staff was doubled to 25 personnel; system analysts, programmes, web developers, graphic designers, taxing and business development officers are the key players. The annual sales exceeded 6-million-pound last year; 40% of sales comes from web development services which is mercers 10% annually, the only area that did not affect due to recent secession.

ABL develops small and medium size websites and offers hosting for the same market. The customers come from a variety of industries including manufacturing, trade and services, the average life of a project is 8 weeks with a standard deviation of 2 weeks that involves about 8-10 personnel. The acquisition team which is also known as business development team responsible for contract winning the specification is agreed/ decided with the help of a developer; the organization has been divided into five teams: web development, programming, texting, maintenance and hosting. Each team is headed by a team leader and all teams are reporting to the chairman, the head of the organization (Exhibit 1).

Exhibit 1 Specification of the proposed website
<ul><li>Overview</li><li>Optimization - accessible, budget of link building</li><li>Number of web pages</li><li>home page, product list, product details pages, on line-shop, about us, contact us, site map,</li><li>Style and layout</li><li>Over all style</li><li>Navigation-links to home page, product list, about us, contact us</li><li>Additional characteristics</li><li>Accessibility- W3C standards</li><li>Valid code - available to w3c specification</li></ul>

The overview must show the purpose of the site; as a sample, it should say "we want people to find out our products by searching the web. The site will provide detailed information about the products and enable visitors to make an on live purchase" (Vordweb, 2010).

ABL received an order of a medium size website to be delivered within four weeks of a trading organization. The customer has provided the list of requirements as shown in Exhibit 2.

Exhibit 2 Requirements of the project
History of the company List of major customers served in the past and some of them are being served The list of major products the company sales A list of the staff in service How the customer can be accessed Organization structure of the company Major links to useful organization Order tracking system Three D display of each product with details of its features <ul><li>Payment and financial issues</li><li>Order or shopping procedures</li><li>Goods selecting process</li><li>Customer services</li><li>FAQ</li><li>Others (if any)</li></ul>

It is the business practice within ABC that a general meeting of all heads of the teams is held upon receipt of a new project which can be called a project initiation meeting. Each project is given a name by the business development team in order to distinguish it from another project. This project has been called as SHARP for this purpose.

The usual meeting was held to discuss SHARP on Monday morning at 10:00. Mr. Farkat, the head of the ABL inaugurated the meeting and introduced the project to the participants, the meeting has held to decide various phases of the project such as conceptualization, planning, execution and termination. In addition, risk identification and management are the part of the agenda. An analysis of the project was undertaken to decompose it into more professional teams. Mr. Kakor, the head of system analysis team identify the details of the project. He proposed a tentative list of the website components as shown in Exhibit 3.

Mr. Faraket suggests formation of a team to oversee the project; the other member agreed with him. A team called SHARP was formed whose members were heads of various team.

It was also decided that the responsibilities will be assigned on the basis of teams rather than individuals; the usual head of the tam will be the coordinator of that particular team. The meeting was adjourned until next day when project will be planned.

Exhibit 3 The components of the website		
Components	Items	%
The title	1	0.3
Number of banners	20	7
Number of text boxes	15	5
Number of marquees	2	0.7
Number of slide shows	2	0.7
Logan of strategic partners and links	7	2
Product categories	4	1.4
Hyper links	180	61
Frames	3	1
Images	50	17
Colours	10	3.4
Total items	294	100

The next meeting held where it was decided that the project will be implemented according to project life cycle approach. PLC according to pm1 consists of four phases; concept, planning execution and termination. There are taken in turn in the following pages.

Project Initiation

Initiation is concerned with identification of deliverable and the benefits associated with the project (Ward and Chapman, 1995); or according to PMI (2010) inputs (product description, strategic plan, project selection criteria, historical information) and output (project charter, assignment of a project manager, constraints, and assumptions). The owners of SHARP decide inputs who would have described the project and apply the selection criteria to obtain the economic justification of the project. ABL should describe the project in order to give it a separate identity; the description of the project in non-technical terms may be as follows.

The project is a website that provides identity to the organization on the web and an instrument for e-commerce and e-business.

The details of the project have been provided in table 2 as provided by the customers concerned. Benefit of the project to ABL is that it would contribute towards the annual revenue and strengthened image of the organization as a leading provider of web services.

Since the organization is a small company and projects it works is also always small or at the most medium size, therefore, imitation of a new project is briefly dealt. Detailed analysis is not made which is usually done in project initiation document (PID) table 3 has been prepared to describe the project.

Project planning at ABL

The objective of planning is to understand the project, the details of the work to be accomplished and the time scale. If provides the basis recourse allocation and commitment of different teams. The work is divided into milestones and teams are establishes, monitoring and control mechanism is defined (Anderen et al, 1995). It may include detailed design, a workable plan and allocation of resources (Ward and Chapman). PM1 provides a more elaborated view of the planning process: scope, activity details, budget issues, project risk, schedule development etc. However, all the components are not applicable to ABL; they are considered in the following paragraphs.

The project team prepared a schedule of milestone and related details. ABL initiate a project when a customer approached for a new job or and his proposal in accepted which as always considered the first milestone. The second is to define the project in technical or professional terms for various teams to understand the requirements. A meeting is usually called to consider the customers' requirements and translate them into specification. Requirement are recorded in Exhibit 2 and the have been translated into specification in Exhibit 3. The third is to allocate parts of the project to various teams and allocate required resources, if they need additional hardware, software, or another requirement. Since almost identical project are done in ABL. A template has been developed for this purpose (See Exhibit 4).

Exhibit 4 Millstone template			
	Deliverable millstone	Completion date	Who is to do
Predevelopment: a-Order b-Definition c-Team formation		Week 1 Week 1 Week 1	
Development: a-Design b-Development c-Programming		Week 2 Week 2 Week 2	

d-Testing Execution:	Week 3	
a-Delivery	Week 3	
b-Implementation to clients	Week 4	
c-System termination	Week 4	

A tabulator depiction of the milestone has been shown in Exbibit 5 when a new project is received in the business development section (team), the team is responsible for negotiation of project price, time scale and delivery mechanism. The team also collects or captures project requirements. Sometimes the customer may not know the characteristics of the website because it is a small organization where these is no IT department or even in some cases any advanced IT literate person. ABL team informs the clients that such and such capabilities can be included in the proposed website. In any case, implementable requirements are collected and to some extent negotiated with the customers. Customer and ABL team agreed about the price of the product.

The milestones in the following table demonstrate various components in more details which guides a project manager over the life of the project. It looks like a road map that helps arrangement of resources at different stages of the project so that planned can achieve its objectives. Predevelopment determines the fate of other milestones because it lays down the foundations for them.

Exbibit 5 Milestones		
M1	**M2**	**M3**
Order (Initiation)	Design	Delivery
Definition	Development	Implementation
Team formation	Programming	Termination
	Testing	
M1=Pre-development, M2=Development, M3 Execution		

The same team defines the project in technical terms principally for development team, but it is exchanged with customers for approval. Mostly the ABL definition remains as it is; modification is needed rarely in very few cases. Anyway, any changes or suggested modification are incorporated in the definition (Merchant, 1985). Thus, the project is defined officially. It is followed by formation of the project team (the details will be discussed later on). Thus, the project is in the hands of the project development team (PDM) which is known with the name of the project, so the SHARP team is responsible of the endeavours. Up to this state the project is known at predevelopment phase.

The development phase will be discussed in the next section and the final phase in the execution. The former is the backbone of the project life cycle because the actual product or tangible deliverable is "manufactured" during the phase. The later deals with client: delivery to the client, implementation of the website on the systems of client and debugging of the website, if it does require.

Project organizing

Organizing refers to the decisions making to determine the arrangement of responsibilities to different individuals, teams or departments. The purpose is to achieve project objective, which resources will be employed to do that. It also includes mechanism for management and coordination of activities (Smith, 2007).

Five key tasks are to be performed under the banner of organizing:

1. Determination of assignments or responsibilities
2. Deployment and estimation of resources
3. Management of all of the above
4. Decision of senior management about the coordination of the project

ABL has a double tier system of arrangement of responsibilities: predevelopment phase and development phase. Business development team is responsible for predevelopment phase, while other teams jointly do development. The customers face team is responsible for delivery and post-delivery phase. It applies the organization structure for the project consists of three teams as shown in Exbibit 6.

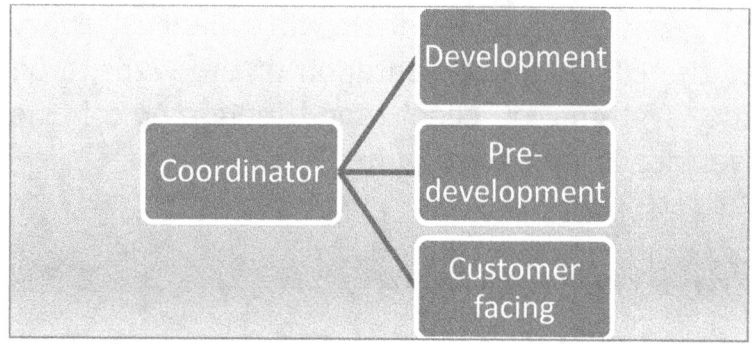

Exhibit 6 Project organization

Each team picks up required people from the organizational teams i.e. designers, graphic or programming. Predevelopment team normally takes a week to negotiate with customer define the project in technical terms for development team and forms a team appropriate with the nature and size of the project concerned. For instance, if the project needs intensive programming skills then two members from the programming team are included in the development work. If above average graphics are required, a graphics intensive team is picked up and so on.

The development team is responsible to design, develop, programme and test the website. There are technical jobs, so IT professionals dominate the team; the coordinator of the project checks the progress on weekly basis. Individuals members of the team remain in touch with each other on daily basis and the developments in the project are discussed as and when they need assistance from one another.

The execution team received the software as a finished product from the development team, however, executors' double checks the functionality and ensures quality parameters. The website is delivered to the customers with help documents and FAQs. A member of the team helps the clients to implement the website; any abnormality is noticed and debugged. When everything works ok, the termination documents are exchanged say the software has been received by the client and is working as agreed initially.

The coordinator oversees all team, nevertheless, the project moves almost sequentially, he should concentrate on one team at a time. Some parallel work is done in development phase when developer, programmers and designers work together. Any changes in design lead to corresponding changes in product characteristics or programmes codes.

Delivery of the product, however, widens the authority of coordinator to outside the four walls of ABL to customers. He ensures the delivery of the project on time and keeps in touch with implementers. Any discrepancy is resolved with the help of business development team who had initially negotiated the characteristics of the website with client as well as technical personnel from various teams from where the project went through. Thus, a project seems to a collected effort of the entire organization rather than expert piece of a single person or a team.

Theoretically, the project sponsor or coordinator encounter two alternatives to organize a project: hierarchical and matrix organization. The later carries a range of benefits: improved communication, flexible organization. Better use of resources, improved decision making and fixing responsibility is easy for managers (Andersen et al., 1995) given that the Exhibit 7 shows the teaming arrangement of SHARP. It looks like a matrix structure. The columns contain the project while the rows indicate the organization teams.

The predevelopment has been assigned to business development team; its functions have been described in the previous paragraphs. All other teams are involved in the development work. However, testing and business development take part in execution due to its nature.

Exhibit 7 Organization of SHARP						
Project teams	**Organization teams**					
	Bus. Dev.	**Design**	**Graphics**	**Systems Analyst**	**Testing**	**Programming**
I	√					
II		√	√	√	√	√
III	√				√	
I- Predevelopment, II- Development, III Execution						

A related issue in project management is preparing a responsibility chart according to mile stones. The project has been divided into ten milestones which are listed above. The next question is to assign each milestone one or more teams to accomplish the job; the Exhibit 8 through light on them.

The purpose of the responsibility chart is to pinpoint the job to be done; the assignment has been made according to teams rather than individuals because ABL is a small organization where teams are material than individuals.

Exhibit 8 Responsibility chart of various milestones

Teams	Milestones									
	Contract	Definition	Team formation	Design	Development	Programming	Testing	I	II	III
1	✓	✓	✓							
2				✓						
3				✓						
4					✓					
5						✓				
6							✓	✓	✓	✓

1-Business development 2-Design 3-System Analysis 4-Graphics 5-Programming 6-Testing

I = Delivery, II = Implementation, III = Termination

Activity chart can augment the above arrangement at greater details. Table 3 shows the components of the proposed website; if we assume each part as an activity than a table can be prepared for them as has been a practice in ABL. Since the website components are selected with development phase, therefore, activity chart of the phase has been included here (see Exhibit 9).

Exhibit 9 Activity chart for design			
Personnel			
Activities	**I***	**II***	**III***
Banners	√		
Text boxes		√	
Slide shows			√
Marquees			√
Frames	√		
Images		√	
Hyper links	√	√	√
Partners logo			√
Product list		√	
Colours	√	√	√
Title bar	√		
Mics	√	√	√
I-Staff 1, II-Staff 2, III-Staff 3			

The workload is divided according to the available time of each person since all personnel work on several projects at the same time. ABL integrates new projects with the existing projects rather than arrangement of a project to

a specific individual or team on full time basis.
(See Exhibit 10 and 11).

Exhibit 10 Millstone and their details			
PHASE	**Deliverable (milestone)**	**Completion date/time**	**Responsibility**
Pre-development	a-Contract approval	Week 1	I
	b-Project definition	Week 1	I
	c-Team formation	Week 1	I
Development	d-Design	Week 2	II
	e-Development	Week 2	III
	f-Programming	Week 2/3	IV
	g-Testing	Week 3	V
Execution	h-Delivery	Week 4	I
	i-Implementation	Week 4	V
	J-Termination	Week 4	I/V

I-Business development team, II-Design team, III-Graphic team, IV-System Analysis team, V-Testing team

Exhibit 11 shows the bar chart of various phases.

Exhibit 11 Phase bar chart				
PHASE	Week 1	Week 2	Week 3	Week 4
Pre-development				
Development				
Execution				

Execution (control)

The first step in execution is to start work as per schedule and monitor whether everything is going as planned. According to Smith (2007) who refers Merchant (1985) in this connection control is "the systematic process through which managers regulate organizational (or project) activities to make them consistent with expectations established in plans and to help them achieve all predetermined standards of performance". Key function to know progress and them take corrective action, if necessary, movement of milestone date, changing objectives, injecting additional resources and rearranging of workload of teams or team member are the possible action that may be taken (Andersen et al., 1995). Ward and Chapman (1995) write that change in design of the project is the key source of project risk. Thus, managing it is important at this stage. ABL executed the project gradually as a part of the day-to-day business. The progress was monitored on weekly basis; a progress report was designed for the purpose. For example, the design team reported the progress of the first week; the progress has been shown in Exhibit 12.

Exhibit 22 Progress report of week 1 of design team								
Personnel	**Activities**							
	Banners		Text boxes		Marquee		Frames	
	Complete	Balance	Complete	Balance	Complete	Balance	Complete	Balance
Staff 1	9	9					3	X

Staff 2		8	7				
Staff 3				2	X		

Staffs 1 is responsible for banners and frames. He has completed half of the banners and all the frames at the end of the first week of project development (note that it is the second week of the project). It means the remaining work is to be completed in the second week of the development (in the third week of the project). Similarly, the staff 2 is responsible for text boxes; he has completed almost half of them and the balance will complete in the forthcoming week.

There are 294 total items in the project (See Exhibit 3), the balance of work and progress have shown in Exhibits 13 and 14.

Exhibit 13 The balance of work remaining at the end of the first week (the second week of the project)			
Activities	**Amount remaining**		**Completed**
Banners	10	50%	10
Text boxes	7	47%	8

Hyper links	80	44%	100
Images	20	40%	30
Logos of strategic partners and their links	3	43%	4
Total balance (No. of items)	120	41%	152

Exhibit 14 shows the remaining work that need to complete in time as planned.

Exhibit 14 The amount of work completed		
Activities	**No. of item**	**Status**
The title bar	1	√
Marquees	2	√
Slide shows	2	√
Product categories	4	√
Frames	3	√
Colours	10	√
Total	**22**	

The total number of items completed was 174; thus 59% of the work has completed and 41% is remaining for the second week. See balance of wok (Exhibit 15)

Exhibit 15   The balance of work (Percentage)

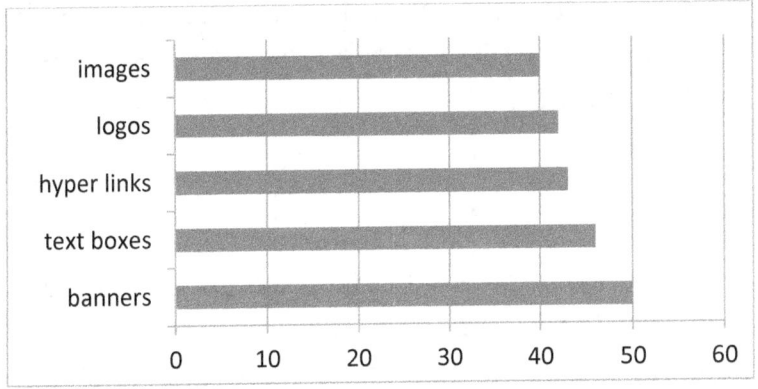

These diagrams are used to control the activities of the project and to monitor the progress. There was no discrepancy in any of the teams or individual; the reports were also sent to management to keep them informed about the status of this particular project as a part of the feedback procedures laid down in the project charter.

It is important to analyse the project at the outset for better implementation. For instance, Table 3 shows the percentage break down of the workload. The analysis is all about development phase for the purpose of this document.

The project was completed in the following week without any impediment and moved to testing team. The test drive was completed as per requirements of the client. The project met its quality standard as outlined by software charted bodies. Since it was ready to be delivered on time, therefore, the manufacturing cost did not increase and consequently the budget was in control. The project moved to the final phase, the termination.

Project termination

Ward and Chapman (1995) believe the phase involves three stages: delivery, service, and support. Delivering of a project includes commissioning and hand over to clients. The product is demonstrated to the customers where a systematic verification is required. In the words of Ward and Chapman (1995) it "involves verifying what the product of the project will do in practice: its actual performance, as opposed to its designed performance."

ABL the project in two steps; a half an hour presentation was given to the director of IT and his team of client organization. The presentation was prepared and presented by business development team and testing team of ABL. They have demonstrated the project electronically where key feature was shown. A session of ten minutes was a part of the demonstration. The software was put on the air, loaded on the client system, and functionality was performed. The IT team was happy with the product, its features and design, the combination of colours and other components.

The second half was to load the website, its various files through the administration box on the same day. All has to be done on Sunday morning so that the new site must be in place by early morning on the following day, the first day of the week. It was done successfully with the help of some personnel of the clients.

The service stage involves a thorough audit of the product, it is documented to know what the achievements, technical and others so that mistake can be avoided and good learning is added to the experience of the individuals and teams worked on the project. The emphasis is on the lessons which are not obvious, so the meanings are identified between the times. ABL conducted such audit offer three days of implementation of the project because it was assumed that the time period was enough to judge the performance of the site and to identify any complicacy in the functionality.

The support stage is concerned with maintenance and liability in the post delivery and service stages. Website maintenance involves uploading information which is time sensitive such as events, circulars and news. It is usually the job of client's web master; however, it may need help of the developer if major changes are to be introduced or hosting is changed. Some developers such as ABL offer periodic maintenance of its client's websites virtually free of charge; the purpose of the strategy is to keep a connection with the customers. And it seems to be a competitive advantage for the organization.

The case study assumes that ABL operates an eight-hour shift from Monday to Friday and employees can be hired in week-ends on over-time basis for which they are paid special rates. The employee agreement has a clause in black and white.

Risk management at ABL

Risk is associated with the uncertainties in the variables of project or parameters of a given venture. Perry (1986) believes project risk may emerge from "failure to keep within the cost estimates, failure to achieve the required completion date, failure to achieve the functional performance." He, however, suggests that individual project managers should develop the list of risks appropriate with their projects. Given that the risk in ABL are little bit different from the above but they are the additional risks or sources of risk since ABL projects are also tend to the basic risks as mentioned above: cost, time, and quality.

Risk may emerge from at least three areas: cancellation of contract, learning of key personnel during a certain project and synchronization of a website with the system of clients. Since ABL's business is all about contracted jobs i.e. every website is developed as a special job or product. The customer has the right to cancel the job up to certain point, for instance during phase1, the pre-development. There are cancellation charges which are covering the risk element. The company loss is psychological, for example, the client might have cancelled the contract due to availability of cheap substitute or the company may have suggested liquidation or bankruptcy. These types of cases are about 2%. ABL has insured such cancellations, thus the financial loss is recovered from the policy. The psychological loss is however, retained since there is little rescue available to manage it. The monthly or quarterly progress reports highlight the reasons for such cancellations with the explanation that there was no financial loss due to these factors. Business development team tries to sign only those projects which are more certain. But human judgment may not be as accurate as a mechanical solution, which, unfortunately does not exist in this particular situation.

The second source of risk is associated with changes in specification or changes in the availability of personnel. Changes in specification are dealt with additional charges or increase in the cost to customer. If also affect the personnel working on the project because they have to change features of the website and also change are to be made in workload and planned activities.

A serious risk arises when some key personnel such as the coordinator of a project leaves the organization or fall sick. The issue has been addressed by making sure that personnel should not leave ABL suddenly, must five at least four weeks' notice in order to make necessary changes in the workload of other employees. The second strategy to address the risk is the integration of new projects into the existing business operations rather than assigning the project to a single team. It jeopardizes the project under consideration and in fact the image of ABL.

Integration is more practicable as Andersen and his colleagues (1995) argue; under this arrangement new projects are added in the workload as a part time ventures. It also reduces the negative impacts of leaving any personnel in the development of a project.

The third category of risk rises in the implementation stage when the new site may not be integrated with the client's IT systems. It may be in the areas of software compatibility or excessive security mechanism in the client systems. The "entry barriers" are removed with the help of client organization. It is followed by audit or service to ensure things are going in order and to identify learning points for future reference and improvement in the process of project lift cycle. The learning is both technical as well as business oriented. The former is later applied in technical issues in the sub segment projects and the later are used for negotiation with potential customer. In this way ABL is a learning organization, a character of the agile project management. Agile projects are least tending to failure as reported by Amber (2008). Exhibit 16 summarizes the risk management strategy of ABL with details of the resources of risk, the way of managing it and the risk management options applicable to each of them.

Exhibit 16 Project risk management strategy in ABL		
Source of risk	Managing risk (who bears the risk)	Risk management option
Contract	Customers	Risk transfer
	Third party	Risk transfer
Changes in specifications	Customers	Risk reduction
Changes in personnel	ABL	Risk retention

Implementation	ABL/Customers	Risk reduction

Case questions

1. Do you think the risk management strategy of the ABL is appropriate if not why?
2. ABL had adopted phase approach for managing risk i.e. risk in conception or imitation, planning, organizing and control. Describe key features of each of these phases.
3. The software project was divided into milestones and activities. DO you think the milestones are suitable for the nature of the project?
4. What are the weaknesses in the management of the project? How can they be overcome?
5. Describe the strengths of the approach management has used to complete the project.

3 SOFTWARE DEVELOPMENT IN EAGLES (SDE)

Software development Eagles (SDE) was setup by three friends studying in the Asian University of Hong Kong in 1995 after graduating.

None of the friends had enough money to invest in the business but they were motivated to some entrepreneurial venture rather than work for the others. They have completed three projects together in the university: system development software engineering and IT project management. Their projects were rated above average by their professors. One of them suggested them to start a software development business after graduation.

SME bank and department of industries, the government of Hong Kong was offering financial support for young entrepreneurs. The three friends who were known as eagles in the university borrowed 2 million from the bank and attended a series of seminars and workshops organized by the department of industries about the formulation and management of new companies. The friends also did work experience in the software house, which was partly managed by one of their visiting professors in the city. It was the time when Chinese were proposed themselves to take over the control of the Island from Briton after couple of years, in 1997.

The friends or eagles assume that there would be room for new entrepreneurs when the government would change hands because many existing businesses will move to London in addition to the ever-expanding Asian markets. Eagles won a contract of development of large website only after two months of incorporation of SDE. Since the project was a large endeavour and had to be completed in 12 weeks' times, the eagles (as the company was famous after incorporation) hired two more system analysts, one of them brought ten years' experience and another have five years' experience in the development field. The names of friends were Lee, Long and Lau. Lee was selected as CEO; Mr. Long took over the responsibility of company secretary and Lau as technical director. This was done for the arrangement of the organization or to fulfil the legal requirement but all the members work as normal on all the projects.

The client firm was called speed property LTD. (SPL); Mr. Lee compiled the requirements of the job (or project for the purpose of this writing) has prepared table to demonstrate and summarized them.

New projects are usually discussed in weekly meetings where progress of existing projects is examined and new are started. A meeting was scheduled on Monday March 21, 2017 to discuss the project; the agenda of the meeting consists of: planning the project, selecting the teams and project sponsors, allocating initial resources, reviewing existing control mechanism for this project and deciding the time frame. (Exhibit 1)

Exhibit 1 The Requirement of SPL project		
S. No.	**Name of Component**	**Number**
1	Index page	1
2	Banners	45
3	Slides	2
4	Marquees	2
5	Frames	13
6	Search (Query box)	1
7	Products	6
8	Services	2
9	Text box	292
10	Hyperlinks	30
11	Colours	2

One of the founders used to be the sponsor of any new project, therefore, Mr. Long, the company secretary was s proposed the sponsor for this project, despite the fact that two of the recent addition to the workforce was more experienced. It was his first major project since the company was formed. He was selected because Lee and Lau had lots of projects to manage and partners believe that "employees" cannot be trusted to assign such kind of responsibility. Long, has been active partner in the projects, which they have completed in the university. However, he was chosen secretary of the company because he was efficient negotiator (probably he was a better negotiator among three friends). A team of four other developers was assigned to him. The team was asked to identify the amount of resources, she needs and their timings so that arrangements can be made for them. The meeting can be made for them. The meeting of friends was concluded after making these important decisions.

Mr. Long called a meeting of his team after four days to examine the project and probably start it formally. Other members of the team were trained in different areas of the website development; Mr. Jones was graphic designer, Mr. Yong was HTML writer, Mr. Shan was business analyst and Mr. Fast was database expert.

The Eagles have the tradition to implement projects according to life cycle approach i.e. project analysis and planning, project organizing, implementation, control and evolution. The last part was used for planning projects in the future because learning curve travels up with the completion of every project. Mr. Long setup a team of two individuals for analysis and planning of the endeavour.

The mini team believed that formal planning methods are not useful for the project since it is not large enough to apply CPM or PERT. They have utilized their experience for planning the website. Both members of the planning team participated in scores of the projects during the course of last ten years or so. They believe the project will be completed within specified time plus 10% discount for unavoidable circumstances.

There were number of issues to address at this stage: determining the duration, sequence and dependencies of activities, allocation of resources and assignments of activities to various teams or individuals, determination of milestones and control mechanism.

Management of the project has been accomplished with the passage of time and with the progress of work.

Since the endeavour will be completed in three months, the duration of activities has been estimated based on the past experience; they are shown in Exhibit 2 below.

Exhibit 2 Duration of Activities (in men-hours)		
Activities	**Code number**	**Duration**
Index page	EG1	4
Banners	EG2	15
Slides	EG3	4
Marquees	EG4	4
Frames	EG5	12
Search (Query box)	EG6	2
Products	EG7	2
Services	EG8	2
Text box	EG9	292
Hyperlinks	EG10	74
Colour	EG11	2

The total numbers of men-hours needed were spread over the life of the project since the project will be accommodated as an addition to existing workload i.e. as a part time endeavour. However individual activities were allocated to all team members. Exhibit 3 depicts the distribution of workload.

Members	Activities' to work	Total workload
Jones	Banners, homepage, slides, and marquees	27
Yong	Text boxes	292
Shan	Hyperlinks and Frames	86
Fast	Colours and search boxes	4
Long	Products and services	4

Exhibit 3 Allocation of activities to team members

In addition to that everyone must know the sequence of activities and dependencies that is helpful to visualize the project over its life cycle. Mr. Long did it for other members and he has drawn it in Exhibit 4.

Exhibit 4 Dependencies of activities

Activity	Predecessor
EG.1	None
EG.2	Eg1
EG.3	Eg2
EG.4	Eg3
EG.5	Eg1
EG.6	Eg5

EG.7	Eg6, Eg4
EG.8	Eg6, Eg4
EG.9	Eg8
EG.10	Eg9
EG.11	Eg10

The table may be the basics of developing the network diagram to depict all the activities (Exhibit 5).

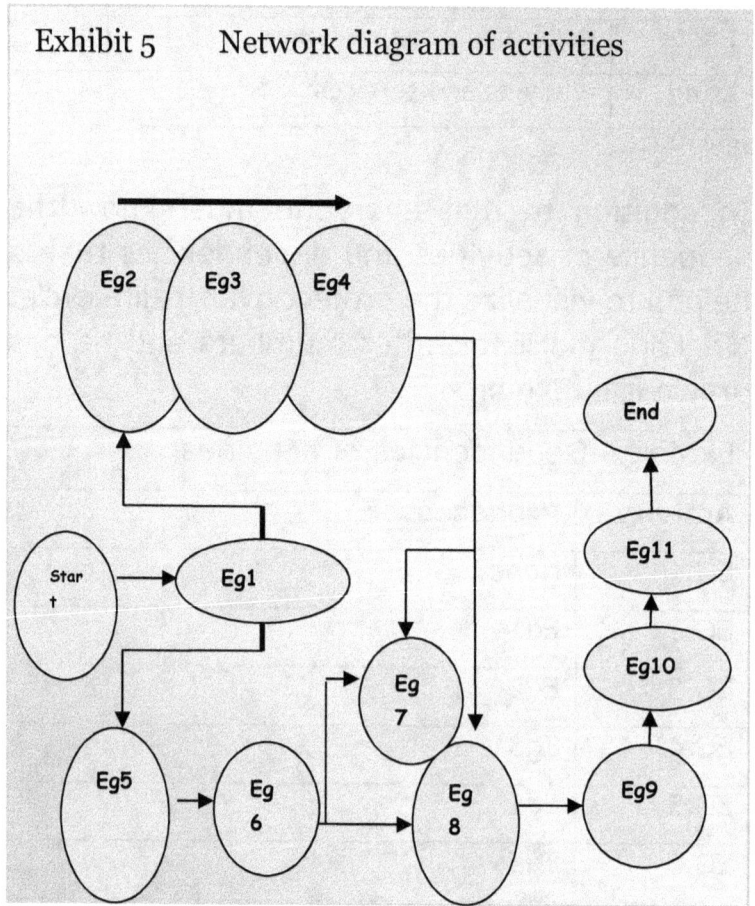

Exhibit 5   Network diagram of activities

Addition of duration of activities helps to determine critical path. Exhibit 6 depicts activities with duration in terms of men-hours required to complete various activities.

Exhibit 6 Duration of activities on the network

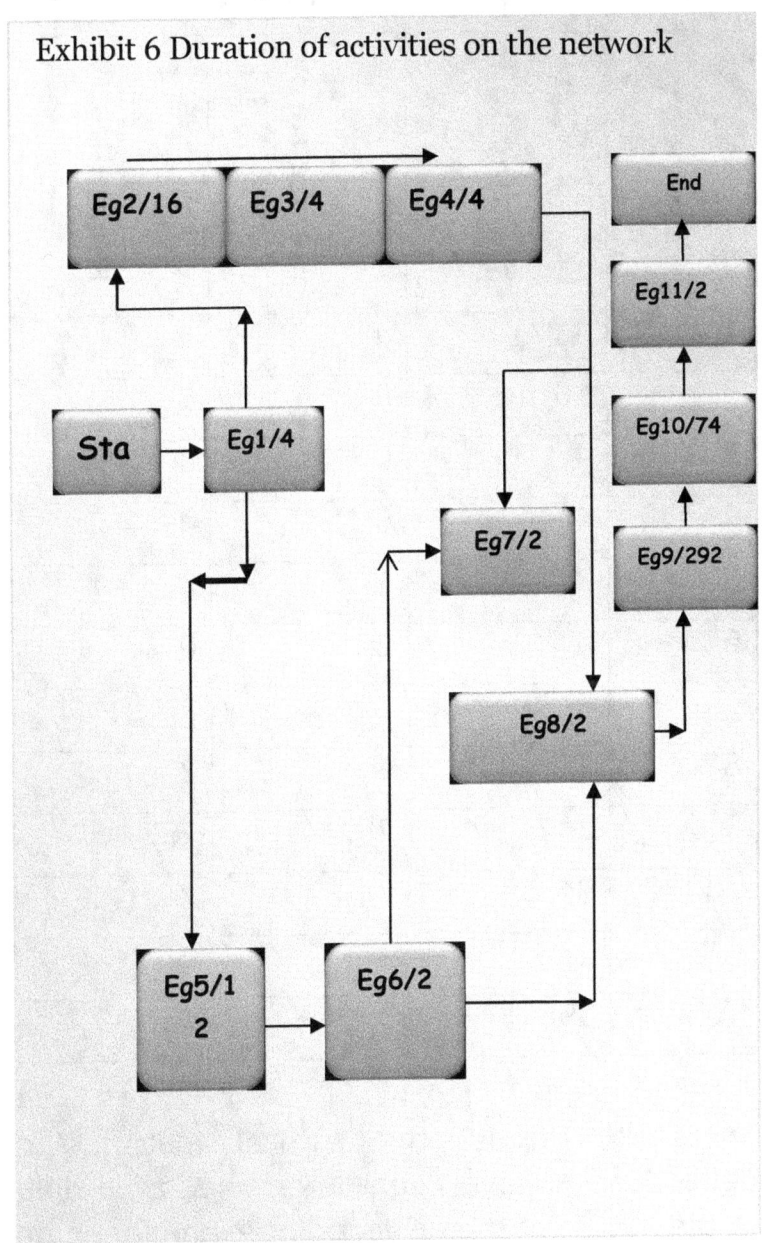

The critical path has been calculated in Exhibit 7. The third alternative is the longest path and takes maximum time to complete.

Activities	Alternative 1	Alternative 2	Alternative 3
Exhibit 7 Calculation of critical path			
1	4	4	4
2	16	0	16
3	4	0	4
4	4	0	4
5	0	12	0
6	0	2	0
7	0	2	2
8	2	2	2
9	292	292	292
10	74	74	74
11	2	2	2
Total	398	390	400

Therefore, it is the critical path. The dependencies have been determined according to the nature of the project. For example, home page is designed so that other features can be created upon it. And the hyperlinks are developed when sub files (supporting files) are created and so on.

Since all the resources for the development of a website are shared; all the members work on more than one project at a time and they use resources as and when they need them. For instance, printers are shared, however each member of the staff owns a PC, which is installed on his desk and dedicated to him. It suggests that no special arrangements are required for the project.

Some project does need new resources but it is associated with the nature of the project. However, budget is set aside for each project for internal evaluation and control purpose.

The length of the project has been determined in man-hours; the calculation of cost is also ascertained accordingly. Each men-hour cost £500 to the company, the cost of each activity is shown in Exhibit 8. Although there are variations in the remuneration of personnel involved yet a flat rate is applied for cost calculation for the sack of simplicity and convenience.

Reporting and Control Mechanism

It is widely believed that planning looks forward and control looks back i.e. what has been done and how that is done. Control involves determining timings of reports and deciding what reports are required to measure the progress of a project. The responsibilities are fixed for the collection of data, analysis, and communication of results to the relevant authorities. The project sponsor is usually the audience of such reports. The team members may prepare the reports or independent parties can be appointed for the purpose.

Exhibit 8 Determination of Cost			
Activity	Duration	Rate	Activity Cost
EG.1	4	£500/men-hour	£ 2000
2	16	"	8000
3	4	"	2000
4	4	"	2000
5	12	"	6000
6	2	"	1000
7	2	"	1000
8	2	"	1000
9	292	"	146,000
10	74	"	37,000
11	2	"	1,000

Total			207,000

The independent parties may be within the organization or external organization may be hired. Sometimes the clients are also involved in the progress monitoring team.

The progress is checked at regular intervals such as weekly, fortnightly, or monthly basis; milestones and or major activities are also feasible in project management. Maturity gates are also applicable in some projects. Eagles use milestones as a principle-reporting event for the project; individual performance is measured for each team member. It is important because team members usually work on more than on project at a time. Therefore, their progress is required. For instance, the weekly performance report for Jones shows the projects on which he worked and the time spent on each of it. (Exhibit 9)

Exhibit 9 Weekly progress report of Mr. Jones			
Projects	Allocated time for the project	Work completed	Work in balance

EG	28 men-hours	4	24
EM	58	12	46
EF	122	2	120
EB	60	10	50
ES	12	12	0
Total	280	40	240

The progress of projects is also reported on weekly basics about the completion of various activities and or if a milestone has been reached. A weekly report has been prepared for the first week of the project under discussion. Exhibit 10 shows the details.

Exhibit 10 Progress report of activities			
Activities Completed	Time worked	Total project time	Balance
EG 1	4 hours		
EG 2	16		
EG3	4		
Total	28	414	386
Total %	7%		93%

The project planning and organizing were completed but the outcome yet to be seen. A number of issues emerged when implementation was on the way to reality. The person in charge of hyperlinks left the company because he has been offered a better position in the neighbouring firm. A new guy was employed to replace him; however, the employment process took four weeks i.e. advertise, screen, interview, select and induct. He was an experience person but unable to cope with the lost time. It caused to delay the entire project by one week and increased the cost by £20,000 which reduced the return on investment below industry level. The customer was compensated for the loss of time with a reduction in the total price of the project; it added another £10,000 to the total cost. In addition, Eagles were unable to start another project which was in pipeline at that particular time. It also created an implied cost that increased the fixed cost related to development of all projects which used to be distributed over all projects in the current financial year. It was the first project since the inception of the company which derailed from the plan substantially. Management believed that it would have far reaching impacts on profitability, productivity and image of the organization. Therefore, a team was set up to identify the causes of delay in addition to the resignation of the person in charge of hyperlinks. The purpose was to redefine the project management strategy in the future based upon the findings of the current experience. The person in charge of the investigation should submit the report within two weeks.

Case questions

1. The project overrun triple constrains i.e. cost, time of delivery and quality. Do you agree? If not why?
2. Does the resignation of the person in charge of the hyperlinks, the only reason of the project delay?
3. What were the other reasons of failure (if any) and how they could be avoided?
4. The company lost money, creditability, and many more assets. What were they? Could they be saved?
5. If you were the person in charge of the investigation team and your research revealed that in addition to the personnel issues, there were project management problems in the case. What amendments do you suggest to be included in the future business or project management strategy?

4 PTCL AND PRIVATISATION OF TELECOM INDUSTRY

1. Telecommunication industry in Pakistan

PTCL was managing the telecommunication sector as a single organization until 2003 when the government deregulated the industry and other companies were allowed to enter the business. Government permitted private investors to open Public Call Offices (PCOs) or cellular services. A number of mobile phone companies started their business after the deregulation. Ufone, Mobilink, WaridTel, Paktel, Telenor and Instaphone are the key players.

Mobilink started operation in 1994 as a subsidiary of Orascom Telecom (OT). Mobilink is the pioneer in cellular business with good infrastructure in place and professional approach to managing the business. It has more than twenty million customers, 54% of market share and reach all over Pakistan. It has laid down an under-sea cable from Karachi to Fujairah and setting up 6000km long optic fibre cable network to meet its demand.

Ufone a fully owned subsidary of PTCL commenced its business in 2001. Its network covers more than 750 cities and the asset based reached to Rs.27 billion during the year 2006. The number of customer also increased dramatically from 2.58 million in 2005 to 6.34 million in 2006. Ufone provides roaming services to 79 countries with partnership of 150 operators worldwide. After-tax profit increased from 61% to 87% in the previous year, consequently earning per share (EPS) boosted from Rs.2.94 to Rs 4.74. The company is expanding its network in order to entertain 10 million customers in the years to come.

Telenor, the European-based smart organization launched its business in Pakistan few years ago. Telenor's services are excellent in some areas such as sound clarity, GPRS connectivity time is less than rival Ufone since is enhanced with EGPRS technology. And its easy recharge ranges from Rs.10 to 1000 with limitless validity. The SMS service is considered satisfactory. However, the international side of SMS is costly and reaches the desired destination with difficulty. The user needs to register with the destination country before sending their massage. A commentator believes that 'Telenor soon will emerge as a big cellular company in Pakistan due to their devotion excellent service'.

Warid Telecom commenced its business in mid-2005; it covers 28 cities and its reach is about 32 million people. It offers cheaper call rates than close competitors like Mobilink, 30 second billing policy and Family and Friends package. Warid is targeting student segment and probably young people's market. The GPRS service is slow and expensive; e-mail is inefficient and slow.

2. Pakistan Telecommunication Company Limited (PTCL)

The PTCL came into being in June 2006 when Etisalat of UAE bought a lion share of the organization. PTCL evolved from a governmental department dealing with postal services to in late forties to the modern telecommunication organization offering state of the art services to its customer. Exhibit 1 sheds light on the key events that lead P & T Department to became telecommunication giant in the country (See Exhibit 2).

Exhibit 1 Evolution of PTCL*

1947   *Posts & Telegraph Dept. established*

1962   Pakistan Telegraph & Telephone Department.

1990-91	Pakistan Telecom Corporation Waiting list: 900,000 Expansion Program of 900,000 lines initiated (500,000 lines by Private Sector Participation 400,000 lines PTC/GOP own resources).
1995	About 5 % of PTC assets transferred to PTA, FAB & NTC.
1996	PTCL Formed listed on all Stock Exchanges of Pakistan
1998	Mobile & Internet subsidiaries established
2000	Telecom Policy Finalized
2003	Telecom Deregulation Policy Announced
2006	Etisalat took over the organization

*Courtesy of PTCL

Exhibit 2   Brief history of PTCL

From the humble beginnings of Posts & Telegraph Department in 1947 and establishment of Pakistan Telephone & Telegraph Department in 1962, to this very day, ours is a story of commitment and vision.

Pakistan Telecommunication Corporation (PTC) set sails for its voyage of glory in December 1990, taking over operations and functions from Pakistan Telephone and Telegraph Department under Pakistan Telecommunication Corporation Act 1991. This coincided with the Government's competitive policy, encouraging private sector participation and resulting in award of licenses for cellular, card-operated payphones, paging and, lately, data communication services.

Pursuing a progressive policy, the Government in 1991, announced its plans to privatize PTC, and in 1994 issued six million vouchers exchangeable into 600 million shares of the would-be PTCL in two separate placements. Each had a par value of Rs. 10 per share. These vouchers were converted into PTCL shares in mid-1996.

In 1995, Pakistan Telecommunication (Reorganization) Ordinance formed the basis for PTCL monopoly over basic telephony in the country. It also paved the way for the establishment of an independent regulatory regime. The provisions of the Ordinance were lent permanence in October 1996 through Pakistan Telecommunication (Reorganization)

Act. The same year, Pakistan Telecommunication Company Limited was formed and listed on all stock exchanges of Pakistan

Since then, PTCL has been working vigorously to meet the dual challenge of telecom development and socio-economic uplift of the country. This is characterized by a clearer appreciation of ongoing telecom scenario wherein convergence of technologies continuously changes the shape of the sector. A measure of this understanding is progressive measures such as establishment of the company's mobile and Internet subsidiaries in 1998.

As telecommunication monopolies head towards an imminent end, services and infrastructure providers are set to face even bigger challenges. Pakistan also entered post-monopoly era with deregulation of the sector in January 2003. On the Government level, a comprehensive liberalization policy for telecom sector is in the offing.

PTCL is in full awareness of the same, and future policies feature a strong conviction of healthy competition.

The company is in process of enhancing organizational and business proficiency through vertical integration and horizontal diversification. At the same time, cross-national ownerships, operations, and partnerships are being evaluated with a view to developing and diversifying the business.

Courtesy PTLC Pakistan.

According to an online source,

PTCL is the leading provider of basic telephone services to the private sector in Pakistan with over 4.4 million telephone lines in service. Besides providing fixed line and ancillary services, PTCL owns Pakistan Telecommunication Mobile Limited, one of five GSM cellular providers in Pakistan and Paknet a countrywide Internet service provider. Its strong financial position demonstrated during FY 2004 excluding subsidiaries as per unconsolidated financials of PTCL indicates: Revenue PKR 74,124 million, Operating profit: PKR: 41938 million, Net Profit after Tax: PKR: 29,169 million, Total Assets: PKR: 141,595 million, Total Equity: PKR: 83,600 million, with a network of installed 5.27 million lines and 4.43 million access lines in service.

The company created and follows an ambitious mission, which says, to achieve our vision by

- an organizational environment that foster professionalism, motivation, and quality.

- an environment that is cost effective and quality conscious.

- services that are based on the most optimum technology.
- 'Quality' and 'Time' conscious customer service and sustained growth in earnings and profitability.

It inspired management and employees to define a revolutionary vision to make the organization a truly 21st century enterprise by taking full benefit of the opportunities revolving around them in the telecommunication sector today. It encapsulates the future vision, which emphasizes the leading role of PTCL in the region through customer care and enhancing the value of shareholders. The company believes that 'to be the leading Information and Communication Technology (ICT) service provider in the region by achieving customers' satisfaction and maximizing shareholders' value' leads its employees towards the target.

To achieve that vision a set of five core values were identified in the ever-changing culture of the enterprise. It includes:

- Professional integrity
- Customer satisfaction
- Team work
- Company loyalty
- Corporate culture

A board of directors consists of nine members (including a chairman) has been set up to manage the business affairs. The chairman is a secretary of ministry of Information Technology of the government of Pakistan.

The organization structure consists of five layers of management: President & Chief Executive Officer (CEO), Senior Executive Vice Presidents (SEVPs), Executive Vice Presidents (EVPs), Managing Directors (MDs), General Managers (GMs) and Chief Engineers (CEs).

GMs are grouped under four geographical areas and CEs are assigned into functional division such as Administration, Maintenance & Operation, Development, Business Development, Business Planning & strategy, International communication and Information technology.

PTCL is serving both corporate customer and end users. It offers toll free numbers, premium rate numbers, virtual private networks, audio conferencing service, televoting and Apnades Calling Card services to the corporate community. DXX Leased Data Circuit & Internet Bandwidth, FLAG (MBS/IP Transit), ISDN BRI (Teleplus), ISDN PRI/E1(Trunk Line), Universal Access Number (UAN) and Universal Internet Number (UIN) are also available. One the company document reads

PTCL is striving hard to facilitate its valued corporate customers at each level of service. PTCL offers a host of unmatched services to suit the needs of the Corporate Customers. The list of Corporate Services is given as under. For more information regarding any of the following services, PTCL Corporate Customer Centres can be contacted (PTCL, online).

The end users are offered traditional telephone services, digital facilities, ISDN BRI and CLI facilities. Customer care has been divided into CLI Binding, bill payment, customer service and complaint numbers, PTCL directory, complaint directory and corporate customer centres segments. Customers tariff have been split up into nine categories: domestic, international, calling cards, international circuits, T.V. channels, radio maritime, call centres, PBXs / PABXs and IP connectivity for international customers.

3. Economic and business environment

Pakistan is taking off as an emerging economic power in the region. The growth rate is around 6% since 2003 when telecommunication sector was deregulated. This study includes the examination of PTCL after government's decision to break the monopoly of PTCL in Telecommunication sector and liberalise the industry. The objective was to attract foreign investors to pure money inward and initiate a healthy competition, the key characteristics of the market economy, the country had adopted since its birth in the late forties.

The telecom sector is expanding (data) and new competitors are emerging, it intensifies the competition. The pricing strategies of various companies are the basis of competition (data). Competitors are using various strategies to capture new customer. (what are those) Main threat is coming from mobile phone companies; they offer cheaper (data) telecommunication services and relatively easy way to get connected with their networks.

PTCL's problems grew deeper when new Long Distance and International (LDIs) competitors entered the market and the company has to surrender its leadership in this segment. However, new management is determined to regain the lost position in the near future by concentrating on this particular area of concern. Management is confident that the regulatory agencies would continue to provide safeguard against unfair market practices (What are those).

Reduction in settlement rates posed another challenge (?). The situation further worsened when Universal Service Fund was imposed (?). It threatened the revenue stream in the following financial periods. Another problem came from increase in the grey traffic. (?)

Rise in operating expenses reduced the revenue receipts and ultimately cut down the amount of profit. It reduced Earning Per Share by 28.23% and pressurised the share prices in the stock exchange as well as shattered the confidence of the shareholders. Revenue reduced by 11.08% in the first nine months of 2005 /06 due to increased salaries, establishment expenses, WLL marketing cost and booking of prior year rental cost.

PTCL in response to the market and competitors has taken a number of measures. The company has expanded its capacity by 1, 182, 000 lines; of which 811, 000 are Wireless Local Loop (WLL) lines. The customer base has been expanded by 209, 000 WLL and 44,000 normal lines. Value added services and Interconnect were enhanced to generate more revenue.

The company moved with laser beams to Giga Bit Technologies, increase global connectivity by 3,000 circuits, able to illuminate more than 10, 000 fibre cables. It runs an international submarine cables system and installed high capacity domestic fibre optics backbone rings. At the regional level, it introduced Internet Dial up Access (IDA) and Universal Internet Access (UIA) in the region.

PTCL is concentrating on its core activities by restructuring in order to improve the quality of services, enhance performance and achieve competitive edge in the industry. In this connection CTI was fully sold out to Siemens AG while proposal is under consideration to sell 71.9% shares of Telephone Industries of Pakistan to another unit of the Government of

Pakistan. (has it been done?) It would provide more time and energy to management to focus on the critical but profitable segments of the organisation.

The company is in strong position to exploit the resources and opportunities available in the telecom sector. It owns a large WLL capacity to attract customer and has the ability and resources to take advantage of high potential of increasing market share in rural and semi-urban markets. Management realises the existence of the opportunity and in the process of defining strategy to use installed capacity.

To maintain the industry leadership and gain a competitive edge a range of strategic objectives were approved at the senior level. Further expansion in the network is in foresight. The purpose is to show the industry that management is ambitious to retake the kingdom in a professional way. Secondly, to further expand the geographical reach of the current operations. Management assumes that the more physical expansion would bring more business and vice versa. Thirdly, a strong presence in the market would create more opportunities in one or more segments of the business.

Management realizes the gravity of the situation and takes appropriate measures to restore profitability and productivity. About 1900 daily wagers of Telecom Foundation and 150 contract employees were lay-off in October 'to observe retrenchment'.

PTCL is operating 3020 digital telephones exchanges along with 3101 Long Distance VHF PCOs. The list of countries on ISD reached a record number of 242 during the period. And 155 customer centres have been established to look after present and future customer. The internet services have been extended to 2063 cities.

Fixed Line Capacity (FLC) reached a record level of 4.94m and the number of telephone subscribers is 3.98m. Total length of Main Fibre Optic Link (MFOLF) reached to 4591 km while Optical Fibre Short Haul Links (OFSHL) has been extended to 159.1 km and Optical Fibre Spur Links (OFSL) achieved 4462.7 km land mark.

4. Customer care strategy

The company believes that "Our strength was giving our customers the digital edge". A new customer care system has been launched in June this year called 'Corporate Relationship System' (CREST), 'Jameel Khawaja Executive Vice President Customer Care PTCL has said that,

PTCL was focusing its attention towards Customer Care and creating relationship with customer was its top priority... due to this system corporate customer would not only lodge their complaints but also see the process involved in their rectification. He said PTCL was further expanding spectrum of services and these state-of-the-art value-added services were being provided on cheap rates. (Business Recorder)

The company has introduced free local call in August 2004 from 12am-6am for end users. To penetrate into the local market aggressively, management announced a further reduction of rates for long distance calls (NWD) in August 2006. It is applicable to PTCL fix, PTCL wireless (V Phone), Assan Phone and PTCL Calling Cards. The Ramadan package was announced in September 2006 to attract the attention of international callers. New connection charges were drastically reduced to achieve competitive edge in the telecommunication industry.

A range of incentives were given to IT industry to promote the usage of the Internet and enhance the profit margin of Internet Service Providers (ISPs) in the country.

5. PTLC and deregulation challenge

The Business Recorder (BR) comments on the strategy of the organization to cope with the threat posed by the deregulation in the following words:

PTCL is in the process of introducing more and more innovative and state of the art valued added service, for better customer facilitation. The Company was fully cognizant of the impending challenges, posed by the deregulation of the telecom sector and therefore was preparing itself to match these challenges befittingly.

PTCL is keeping an eye on the illegal telephone exchanges operating in the country in an attempt to take the benefits of deregulation to common people. Many such telephone exchanges have been confiscated. A new national telephony number plan was announced in February 2004. According to the plan the country has been divided into 99 Number Plan areas (NPAs). The details have been given in the following abstract from the BR record.

PTCL is implementing a new National Telephony Numbering plan, approved by the Pakistan Telecommunication Authority on February 6, 2004. The existing numbering plan, which is being changed, needed rationalization to cater for the needs of new operators in the deregulated era as well as the requirements of the future new services. The new numbering plan is based on a uniform 9-digit numbering scheme with two patterns i.e., a 2-digit Area Code for heavily populated areas plus a 7-digit Subscriber Number or a 3-digit Area Code for less populated areas plus a 6-digit Subscriber Number; making a total of 9-digits in both cases.

The plan streamlines the numbering system and reduces the number of area codes from 249 to 99, virtually each district has been assigned a single number to be operated in its geographical territory.

One of the senior engineers Mr. Shakeel Ahmed was asked what was the biggest challenge after deregulation. He replied the cellular phone companies. He said it takes time for PTCL to install infrastructure because laying down cables, exchanges, PCO's etc. is a time ensuring venture. Installation of infrastructure is not viable everywhere; new exchange can be constructed where people live together i.e. in villages and virtually where there is present or potential market for the product we offer. On the country, the cellular phone companies install one pole / tower or distribution centre which serves in a wide area irrespective of pattern of population i.e. living together in clusters or is scattered. The hardware prices are constantly falling that enable even small investors to enter into the cellular business. The entry into the telecom market was used to be difficult due to large infrastructure requirements and associated huge investment. However, in recent year availability of cheap Chinese hardware made it possible to enter the market relativity easily. Consequently, the tariff of both fixed lines and cellular services came down sharply.

The operating cost of cellular companies is nominal whereas PTCL has to make huge investment in hardware and needs more people to run the facilities. The private operators lease lines from PTCL and hire few people to run the facilities. PTCL has to lease the line to these companies since it is a part of the deregulation policy.

Although the Quality of voice of PTCL protocols is very good but customers are price conscious rather than quality. They are happy with bad voice but low price. PTCL has not capitalized this aspect of its product. So Many users do not know the difference; competitive are taking benefits of this ignorance while PTCL not.

To manage the challenge of deregulation PTCL has introduced a range of new products. The most successful of them was WLL technology and its related services. It helps the company to generate revenue over the long run.

5.1 What PTCL is doing to cope with the post deregulation scenario?

Management perceived the heat of it and of monopolistic position in the telecom industry and responded with a range of measures in customer service, new product development, extension in infrastructure, private sector partnership and rationalization of marketing, HRM, public relation and strengthening networking. Reduction in installation charges tariff for voice service and IP bandwidth; it has doubled the collaboration with private sector during type first year of deregulation; introduce new value-added services such as lower denomination prepaid cards, phone bill payment service, prepaid telephony, longer duration local calls, provision of facilities to new entrants and developments of new technologies. Like WLL and IP in the access loop.

PTCL has introduced / launched a number of new product; prepaid calling cards, Aasan prepaid telephony, local call offers, phone bill cads, electronic bill payment facility; installation of submarine cable and other elements of infrastructure.

Ufone and Paknet have been restructured and CTI and IP have been sold to siemens and government of Pakistan respectively.

5.2 Impacts of the above measures

There was no big challenge at the end of the first year of deregulation. PTCL increased revenue by 10.3 % despite of reduction in tariffs. Net profit and dividend went up by 29.17% and 25.5% respectively. However, the second year of deregulation indicates beginning of a new era characterized with high growth in the market, large new investments and latest technologies. PTCL could not capitalize its huge infrastructure, know-how and presence in the market since long time. Consequently, revenue only increased by 2.5% as against 74.12% last year, profit after tax decreased by 8.8 % as against increase of 29.17 %, other financial indicators also suffered setback. It is due to many reasons: nationwide dialling tariff reduced by 46% international outgoing by 22%, internet protocol (IP) charges reduced to $2000 as against $3,950. Thus, PTCL is market share in international incoming calls reduced to 60%.

Following an uncertain situation of privatization during the third year of competitiveness, the company maintained the leading position in the industry despite of reduction in profit after tax by 21.9%, loss of some market share in long distance and international (LDI) segment. Significant was experienced in WLL where it possesses 60% of the market share and increased subscribers base in cellular sector by 190%

Case Questions

1. Can you identify what measures PTCL have taken which can be categorized as PLANNED CHANGE. Support you answer with specific examples discussed in the case study?
2. If you are appointed as a manager of strategic change, what lessons you can learn from the CONTEXT of the organisation. How

would you use the context to design a change programme? Which aspects are more important and why?

3. Contingencies or more specifically the circumstances within which PTCL is functioning are conducive for the kind of change CONTINGENCY theorists suggest. Do you think such a strategy is more pragmatic for the organisation? Why and why not?

4. "Empowerment is commonly a fundamental part of the prescription, offered to improve business performance" Evaluate the statement.

5. Planned change, contingency theorist and contextualists believe that the focus of change is a functional area whereas process-based models assume the unit of improvement is a business process. Which view is more coincide with the contemporary business environment? And why? Give examples from the PTCL situation.

6. Mr. AK Bahraam, the director of Finance, participated in a monthly meeting of head of various departments, Ali Khan the manager in charge of Quality of services or customer services suggested introduction of TQM to improve overall performance and enhance customer services. Mr. Yar Ali, the director of HRM said, "TQM takes second place in the process of shedding a significant number of jobs". He further committed that we had already fired hundreds of daily wagers; many

papers commented that we are deterioration employment situation in the country. Implementation of TQM would further worsen the rate of unemployment. Therefore, TQM is not feasible for PTCL. Do you agree with Mr. Yar Ali? What could be the reasons for which Ali Khan is proposing the introduction of TQM?

7. According to Burns (2004) "Structure and operation of an organisation is dependent ('contingent') on the situational variables it faces – the main ones being the environment, technology and size". It implies that technology is something, which needs to be controlled / managed in order to make the change happen. On the other hand, technology is a key enabler in BPR initiatives. Suppose your Assistant Vice President in charge of strategic evaluation of opportunities and threats requires you to prepare a report to evaluate the competing role of technology in a future change programme in which technology can be a facilitator or an inhibitor. Which type of change initiative would you recommend on the basis of your analysis?

5 LASANI & COMPANY (PVT) LTD

Lasani was established in 1990 as a family business by its current CEO Mr. A. Lasani; the company is dealing with industrial components used in textile plants. It employs 120 personnel in five departments. The pre-tax profit for the last year was Rs. 20m which was 10% less than the previous year. The financial results were a concern for the management; the CEO called a meeting of five directors of various departments in order to discuss the matter and design a strategy to address the issue.

According to schedule Mr. Lasani is supposed to attend the meeting with directors of five major functional areas: marketing, HR, IT, Finance, and Logistics. The agenda for the next meeting was drafted by a team of three members of the above functions excluding IT and logistics since these areas were confronting problems: marketing was complaining about low level of customer satisfaction as revealed by an independent survey published in a respected magazine last month and sponsored by the organization. The director of HR was concerned about the employee turnover rate, the highest in the industry, the director of finance who is a graduate of LUMS and had been working in various capacities in national and international organizations identified a low inventory turnover during the last quarter in which EID-UL-FITR was celebrated for the first time in his career in the organization.

The meeting started at 10:00 am sharp, Mr. Lasani inaugurated the proceeding by saying that we have to identify the causes of these issues so that a contingency plan of action should be prepared before the end of the current financial year which is also a colander year i.e. starting in January and ending in December, six months were remaining in the current financial year. Mr. Kirmani the director of marketing believes that the best way to address these issues was to introduce a contingency change initiative whereas Mr. Khanan the director of HRM suggests a context-based model to resolve the problems. They exchange their arguments in a friendly conversation in the middle of the meeting:

Kirmani: the contingency change gives us an opportunity to integrate our resources with the circumstances such as competition, low demand, and so on.

Khanan: well, I agree with you, but without considering the historical development of our problems, how can we diagnose the real reasons of these issues.

Kirmani; since our structure and operations are different from other organizations we can design a tailor-made solution which will be more suitable for our circumstances.

Khanan; the structure and operations can be accommodated in the content of the new strategy. The content will be translated into a process, the improved way for implementing the strategic change.

Mr. Lasani interrupted their conversation and suggested that it might be a good idea if both of you prepare a short report in support of your proposals, which we can consider tomorrow at the same time. Mr Kirmani and Khann agreed and the meeting was postponed till the next morning. However, it put both Mr. Khanan and Mr. Kirmani's reputation at risk. Both were thinking what to do. What should be the contents of the required proposals and how the opponent can be satisfied?

Case questions

1. What recommendation would you like to extend to Mr. Kirmani and what will be your arguments to be included in the required report?
2. How you would satisfy Mr. Khanan to relinquish his viewpoint?

6 NORTHERN CEMENT LTD (NCL)

The NCL was established in 1976 as a limited company to manufacture high quality cement based on the advanced technology. The entire manufacturing process was computerized in the late 1980's. Computers are used to receive raw material, monitor manufacturing processes and oversee output. The distribution to various B2B and B2C customer is also managed by technology. The internal and external documentation also depends upon the internet-based transmission such as e-mail and Electronic Data Interchange (EDI).

The UNIX and Dos were principal operating systems until 1995 when Windows95 took over as a sole operating system. Databases were integrated to support the new operating systems. The company was using computer aided manufacturing (CAM), Ms Office, coral draw and other software.

PC gained popularity in the company during mid 1990s when offices were equipped with Pentium computers, 15" inch monitors, and HP laser printers. A LAN was set up to provide centralized services to the users. A 5MB internet connection was leased/ hired to support the entire organization.

Mr. A. R. Khan was heading the IT/IS function, which was responsible to look after the IT infrastructure, network and support users. He has also been a member of the team called mini strategists that consists of all middle managers such as director finance, marketing, production and HRM. They used to meet once a month in order to monitor the performance of their functions, achievements of people and address any concern.

The company installed Windows XP in2003 in an attempt to improve speed and lock or interface of screens. Thirty percent of hardware was PI, 30% PII, 30% PIII and 105 PIV. They were equipped with various amount of RAM (Random Access Memory), the most suitable combination when they were acquired. For example, PI came with 128 RAM, PII with 256 and PIV with 512.

In a recent monthly meeting, the functional heads complained about the speed of information systems since computers are taking more than double time to process large files and downloading time also soar. Many users, according to them said, "When I open more than one program, the machine processes very slowly and often shut down or ask to do so". Mr. Khan, the head of IT used to put forward a proposal for replacement of old machines to synchronize the entire system. However, financial constraints did not allow him to implement his intentions. The manager HRM suggested that if RAM was upgraded to 512 to all the existing PCs than these problems may be resolved. The manager marketing said, "The issue may be addressed by replacing PI, PII, and PIII with P4 machines. The director of Finance put forward the idea that all old staff must be replaced with P4 due systems and LCD display.

Case Questions

1. What is the real issue(s)?
2. What causes speed and how that maybe addressed?
3. Various manager put forward suggestion to address the problem, which one is viable and why?
4. Do you think any other solution other than those mentioned in Q.3 above? Prepare a report to defend your view point.
5. If you were the head of IT, what was your reaction to the problem as a professional?

7 PTCL AND COMPETITIVE EDGE

PTCL evolved from a governmental department of post and telegraph in 1947 to a telecom giant in 2006. When Etisalat took over its management, the telecommunication industry was deregulated in 2003 to eliminate the monopoly of one player and to encourage healthy competition. It resulted in expansion of TC industry, was a source of inflow of foreign investment and growth of tele-density in the country.

The greatest strength of PTCL is its infrastructure that emerged as a continuous input from the government over the period of about sixty years. Telephone lines, exchanges, base stations, experienced human resources and other resources are owned by the enterprise. It provides / allows private companies to utilize its infrastructure to provide telecom services to the masses.

The profit margin started to dip since 2004 due to intense competition, since many new players entered the market mainly from international market. The completion is in the cellular phone area because, according to one engineer at the head quarter in Islamabad, Mr. Shakeel Ahmed, it takes time for PTCL to lay down cables, exchanges and PCO's etc is a time-consuming job. The new exchanges can be constructed where people live together or where there is a present and potential market exists for the product we offer. On the other hand, cellular companies install one pole/ tower which serves in a wide area irrespective of pattern of population i.e. living together in clusters or is scattered. He further said that the hardware prices were falling and it makes easy for small investors to enter in the market, the cellular sectors. The entry in the telecom sector was usually difficult due to requirements of large investment and infrastructure.

PTCL introduced many new products and customer care strategies to meet the challenge of deregulation. The wireless Local Loop (WLL) is a fixed line based technology. The customer buys a handset to plug in the power socket and is connected with telephony and the internet periodically to keep the phone line alive. The card is provided by the service provider such as PTCL. PTCL has a 60% share in this area.

PTCL's wholly owned subsidiary Ufone is doing well, its customer base is improving and profitability gaining ground. The earnings of Ufone is contributing positively in the success of both Ufone and PTCL.

PTCL also introduced customer care services where customer queries are answered and their complaints are resolved. The number of customer care centres has been increased to improve the service base.

Some experts believe that the company has a huge infrastructure that can be used to gain competitive edge in the telecom sector. However, the company is not fully capitalizing its strength.

Case Questions

1. One official of PTCL that quality of our sound, one of the success factors in telephone, is better than others but people do not care about it. They want to get connected cheaply irrespective of quality of voice. Do you think PTCL official is right by simply saying that the quality of voice is better than others? What other factors may contribute to realize quality of telephony?
2. According to resource-based view of organization, the more the immoveable resources a company has, the more competitive it is and vice versa, Comment.
3. How PTCL can improve competitiveness with the existing resources? Give example.

8 INFORMATION BASED DECISIONS

Refaan Pakistan was set up in early 1960, the era if industrial boom in the history of Pakistan. The socio-economic stability attracted many overseas Pakistanis to pour their money. A group of investors from Western Europe and United States (US) installed a big industrial unit in Faisalabad. Refaan was established as a limited company to attract local and foreign capital.

Maize was the principal raw material of which more than hundred products are made. Corn oil and Energile are well known in the consumer market while other products are also well taken in the respective markets. The company makes handsome profit since its inception and its products are famous for quality and taste.

Information system department is a small part of Refaan responsible for provision of information to management for structured, semi-structured and unstructured decisions. Periodic reports are produced for this purpose. Some DSS models were also developed that are applied in decision making once and again. One of such models, corn predictors, has been designed to forecast usage, availability and price trends. Exhibit 1 depicts the national production, usage of corn by Refaan and price over last seven years.

Exhibit 1 National production, usage by Refaan and price over last seven years			
Year	National production (tons)	Usage by the organization (tons)	Price/ton (Rs.)
2013	25,00,000	500,000	4000
2014	26,50,000	525,000	4500
2015	24,00,000	524,000	4600
2016	24,50,000	530,000	4800

2017	25,00,000	530,000	4800
2018	23,00,000	535,000	4900
2019	25,00,000	530,000	5000

The trends in all the three parameters are almost steady, only prices are increasing lightly but they are predictable.

The production in 2007 went down sharply to 2,000,000 tons whereas Refaan's management decided to export corn oil, the main product, to some Asian and African countries due to high profit margin. This means additional raw materials will be required for both domestic and export markets. It was estimated that Refaan would consume 700,000 tonnes in the year 2007. This coupled with the fear that the domestic production of maize will remain about same in the financial year 2007 / 08. The company bought 200.000 tonnes extra maize to cope with the changed situation at of 7000/ ton.

The production in the following year went to normal 2,500,000 tones and prices went down to Rs.5000/ton. Meanwhile harvest of maize in

Africa caused two countries to cancel their orders of corn oil. They were using corn oil for industrial use. Additional production in the respective countries increased the production of corn oil in their countries.

Refaan bought 170,000 tons of maize which cost them Rs. 850 million and storage cost went to Rs. 1million. It increased operating cost by 7% and consumed profit by 2% in the financial year June 2007-May 2008.

One of the senior director, Mr. Alladeen was angry with the IT/IS department for the loss of project and soaring of operating costs since IS did not provide right information for making appropriate decisions.

Case Questions

1. What was wrong with the decision and what role IS could play to prevent the situation?
2. Mr. Alladeen's concerns were based on the outcome of a decision. Did he have a right to say that IS did not give appropriate suggestions?
3. Does information system play any role to retain foreign orders or over purchase of raw materials? Propose a report to support your view.
4. Do you think information system (IS) is useless in the situation like for

collecting, processing, and communicating information to various stakeholders?

9 CENTRAL ASIAN AIRWAYS CORPORATION (CAAC)

The Central Asian Airways Corporation was set up after 9/11 when many airliners went to bankruptcy due to low rate of air travel. However, this trend did not continue for a long time since Asian economies were doing very well. A group of them was called Asian tigers. The newly independent states of Central Asia, because of the dissolution of the former Soviet Union, were also taking off. It increased the air travel in Asia and in The Far East; a group of small airlines were merged to form a bigger CAAC with a head quartered in Karachi. Mr. M.B. Siddiqui took charge as a CEO who served in the Gulf air, PIA and QATAR AIR for 21 years in various capacities. He was a deputy to CEO of QATAR AIR when approached and appointed as a CEO of CAAC in 2002. he put the airlines on the way to success by competitive prices and high quality of customer services. Glimpses of financial statements have been shown in Exhibit 1.

Exhibit 1 Financial Statements of 20016-2020					
	2016	2017	2018	2019	2020
Sales (in Millions)	200	205	210	225	235
Cost of sales	160	170	180	190	200
Gross profit	40	45	30	35	35

Mr. Siddiqui left the organization because of personal reasons in early 2008 and the board of directors appointed one of their members, Asif Jan, as a new CEO.

Mr. Jan was an enthusiastic person with a diverse experience in many industries, manufacturing and service. He was concerned about the deteriorating gross margin, unproductive increase of sales any many management concerns. He reviews the operations of the airline and learned that fine routes out of 35 were running in loss, five were at breakeven, 10 were above average and remaining were earning average. He decided to share the information with the board of directors agreed with his proposal to discontinue five suits suffering losses and suggest many measures to improve the suits which were on border line.

There was a consensus about the discontinuation of products/ suits suffering from losses but the board was divided about the products at break-even. One group of directors said, "There should be discontinued straight away because there was a little chance of improvement. Another group argue that since they are covering fixed cost and helping us to provide employment to some workers, we can try to improve them to the extent where they may pick up project somewhere during the forthcoming financial year". The CEO agreed with the second proposal and decided to continue "on the border line" products for another year.

The CEO also formed a team to look into the ways these products can be improved and make them, Mr. A.Y. Burhaan called a meeting with team members from production and marketing departments. MR. Burhaan was originally an accountant but promoted middle management for his deep analytical quality and experience in selling product prices. One of the team member said, "We need to analyse price, volume sold, cost (fixed and variable) and substitutes available ". Another member said, "We will have to analyse marketing strategy of these products".

Case Questions

1. Do you agree with the discontinuing decision of products which were in loss?
2. The product at break-even was continued and a strategy was to design to improve them. Given the arguments of two team member, what can be the components of the proposed or possible strategy?
3. Break-even is related with cost-volume-profit analysis. How these elements are related with a marketing strategy can be formulated and implemented for those products that were making no profit in the product portfolio of the organization under consideration? Give solid arguments in support of your suggestion?

10 INFORMATION SYSTEM AT TAXILA HERITAGE

There were many separate organizations in Taxila to preserve national heritage such as Gandharah Civilization, Buddha's History Museum and Loke Virsa. They were employing 87 people and cost more than a million rupees. Mr. Gohar Ali Marwat was appointed the district commissioner (DC) in 2003. He wanted to improve the local environment by employing more people in the sanitation departments of the city. However, additional budget was not available and district government was not allowed to levy any taxes. Mr. Marwat was capable to save money from the existing budget by reducing expenses on any existing project. The three organizations mentioned above to preserve local cultural heritage were funded partially by provisional government and partially by the district administration. Mr. Marwat called a meeting of the heads of these organizations to discuss the possibilities of merging of these organizations to improve the quality of the heritage service and reduce expenses. The saving was intended to spend on pacing 80 additional garbage bins and to increase the frequency of disposing them on weekly basis.

Mr. Marwat was an IT graduate from Imperial Collage London. He believed that the status of Buddha and related stone-based or hard items can be put on large LCD screens for display. The visitors can browse them to see them in turn or in groups. The customer service representative can help those visitors who do not use computers. These representatives also help users of the computers.

The heads of three organizations agree to form a new organization, Taxila Local Heritage (TLH), TLH came into being in early 2005 with 60 people. Other 27 employees of old three organizations were retired with handsome gratuity and pension benefits.

The new company invested Rs. 500,000 on IT hardware, software and training of employees. An IT section was set up with five persons to work. Their job was to take state of the art #d images of all hard items, statues, household items and their remaining and samples of soil. Flash and Windows media player and other software were installed to run short-term time videos and clips. The 3D image processors were demonstrating respective images like a real one. Some customer commented, "The images are more attractive, beautiful and easy to access than the real-time and real item observation". The real/ actual items were packed and stored and kept in a safe store. The visitor can view them with a special request and additional fee to pay. The 3D images were used to print colour post cards, birthday cards, anniversary cards, marriage cards and Eid cards etc. they were also sold in full albums.

The computerization of heritage material increased revenue the company made profit first time in the history of old three organizations. The profit was reinvested, distributed to employees and apportion of it was transferred to environmental department. The department brought additional garbage bins and increased the frequency of picking/ collecting them to make the city cleaner and more environmental friendly.

Case Questions

1. Do you think computerization of the new organization was the only option available to Mr. Marwat. If not, what were other alternatives?
2. What are other ways of promotion of TLH? For example, print media, electronic media and the web. If you were the manager of the organization, which one would you like to prefer and why?

3. As an information system student, how would you apply the learning from this case coupled with the material you have learned in the text?
4. How would you like to divide the information system of TLH into Marketing Information Systems and a general information system?

11 PROFESSIONAL BOOK PUBLISHING BUSINESS

Professional Books Limited (PBR) was established in 1980 in Lahore. The objective was to provide a state of the art services to growing number of readers. The company was organized as a private limited company with four directors and a managing director. Mr. Ladyanvi was the owner and the managing director and his four sons were directors. PBL inaugurated its first store on March 1980 with an investment of PK10m.

Professional Books Limited (PBL) Lahore was a chain of 11 book store all over Pakistan with branches in major cities. The company aimed at providing professional services to educational institutes, academic and students. The company was organized into four divisions: Natural Sciences, Business and Economic, Languages and Social Sciences. Each division was organized around four departments: professional, academic institutes, students and general readers.

The company advertised in national newspapers and magazines to introduce in the market.

Leaflets, broachers and flyers were distributed in the institutes of higher education in Lahore. The arrangements were made with local and international publishers and distributors for the supply of required inventory.

The company earned a net profit of 12% at the end of the first calendar year. A large number of external orders came from Karachi; therefore, management decided to open another branch in the city with the same supply chain and marketing strategy as she applied in Lahore. The second year was a successful year when the net profit went to 15% including new branch.

PBL opened branches in five other cities including Islamabad, Multan, Peshawar and Queta. Combined profitability went to 20% in 2001, and PBL employed 85 people in all branches.

However, problem started to emerge in 2002 when sales reduced to 90% of the 2001 level and profit went down to 17% against the previous year. But management was complacent about the net profit because PBL was still earning 3% above the industry average. The major changes were felt in 2004 when net profit reduced to 2%, and sales reached to 30% of 2001 level.

Mr. Ludyanvi called an emergency meeting of directors and senior managers to discuss the matter. Mr. Brochi was the director of sales and marketing, said, "The problem lies in our supply chain because we do not have enough inventories to fulfil customer orders timely". Mr. Garjani, the director of HR argued that the problem resides inside the human resources because no new personnel were hired since last four years and no formal training has been conducted during the period. Some more views and arguments were put forward. The managing director decided to hand over affairs of the business to a professional person. Mr. Y. Lakahni was his hotel fellow in an international book fair in London in 2003 and was managing a small book publisher and distributor in Karachi. Mr. Ludyanvi decided to appoint him as a CEO of PBL. The purpose was to inject new blood in the circulation system of PBL in order to come out of the current situation.

Mr. Y. Lakhani took charge of the company in 2005 as a president and CEO. He has experience in publishing and marketing; he has been a production engineer for seven years in Feroze books publishing (pvt) Limited based in Lahore. He took an MBA in evening program at LUMS in 2002 and promoted to middle management soon after his graduation. He improved company's image as a professional publisher who had a track second of earning above average in the industry.

Mr. Lakhani was a target of PBL due to his enthusiasm, experience and ability to convince his counterpart in negotiations. Mr. Lakhani examined PBL strategy, marketing approach and customer relationship as well as production systems/ processes in order to formulate or redesign these elements. He believed that production, marketing and customer relations are the back bone of an organization.

The CEO was surprised to know that there was little investment in IT and information systems since last four years. No hardware or software were replaced or upgraded during the period and website of the parent company is not updated regularly. Thirty percent of customer queries are related to availability of a certain item or its latest edition. Forty percent of the inventory was published before year 2000. The balance is dominated with editions up to 2005 and an insignificant number belongs to 2006-2008. The number of copies available was 2/3 which causes institutional buyer not to place an order. The order processing cycles was four weeks since the payment is received through demand drafts, postal orders and check. They take time to clear. Thus, orders were not processed quickly.

The CEO was concerned about the quality and functioning of MIS that may be instrumental to improve the order cycle tie, the volume of sales and ultimately the competitiveness.

Mr. Lakhani hired his old friend Mr. Daudi who did his masters from the University of London in

2000 and joined Feroze Books in the same year as a head of IT. He improved the department from a support service provider to a strategic partner. Mr. Daudi was also short listed by PBL for the position of CEO but Mr. Lakhani obtained moral support of some unknown person for reaching the position. Mr. Daudi was promoted to deputy CEO in PBL in addition to his usual position as head of IT. Mr. Daudi supposed to analyse the current situation designed a strategy and implement it to overcome current weakness and became a benchmark organization in the book trade/ publishing industry.

Case Questions

1. What should be the strategy of Mr. Daudi to address the situation?
2. What are the professional bottlenecks in the current business approach of PBL?
3. What measures should be taken to improve the unknown characteristics of existing MIS of PBL?
4. Whether a new MIS strategy is required to cope with the user or current strategy may be augmented?

12 NORTHERN ROCKS (NR), PAKISTAN LIMITED

Northern Rocks was established as a public limited company in year 2000 with a paid-up capital of Rs. 200 million. The purpose was to manufacture high quality construction material and distribute it through modern marketing channels. A new website was designed to provide information to customers, receiving orders and tracking orders. Electronic payment system was incorporated in the website to press order within three days. NR offers free delivery within ten kilometres radius of its manufacturing facilities. Long distance orders are also delivered for nominal charges. Since the quality of its products is above average, the prices have been set accordingly.

Northern Rocks is a manufacturer of building material such as tiles, bricks, blocks and related material. The annual sales reached Rs. 200 million in 2007 and profit 20 million after tax in 2000. The company has been organized into four divisions: marble and tiles, bricks, blocks and stone crushing. Figure A shows the organizational structure.

A consultant was hired in the middle of 2001 in order to design an IT infrastructure. He argued that there should be four systems, one for each of the divisions. Management agreed and allowed him, to start work on the project.

All four systems were operational in the beginning of 2002. Systems were working well until 2004 when new president took charge of the Northern Rocks because of sudden death of the previous president. The new president, Mr. A.Y. Jadoon was famous for transformation initiatives.

He started a change initiative where HR was reorganized because the size of the entire business is not so large that the company should be divided into divisions. Since each division was headed by a M.D. and Marketing, Finance, HRM, Production and IT department were run in each of the divisions. The president argued that it was a duplication of activities which cost the company about Rs. 25m. Consolidation of the company into one organization can save up to Rs. 20m, which is directly proportional to the pre-tax profit. Even after paying 40% flat tax, the company may be able to save Rs. 12m.

The decision was happy news for finance since Rs. 12m is being added without any additional investment. Nevertheless, it complicates the problems for IT department who will have to integrate four systems into one grand system. The new system must serve all the departments (old division) as an integrated and efficient system.

There were two tasks for the director of IT services: to accumulate staff from all the divisions without lying off any employee because the Union agreed on the consolidation on the ground that redundant employees will be retrained (if necessary) and redeployed. The second, to keep the features and functionality of divisional systems and merge them into a bigger but consolidated than the old system.

The head of IT, Mr. K. Chaudary called an emergency meeting of senior personnel of IT and brain stormed about what to do. Mr. R. Rukh, head of one of the old divisional IT function said, "Consolidation of old systems is a cumbersome and time-consuming job, instead we can design a new system incorporating features of all old systems". Mr. Chaudary said, "We can integrate old systems into a new one with team work and with expertise of our available staff". Many other participants supported his suggestion. Therefore, he set up a team of four heads of IT departments in their divisions and decided to head the team himself. He asked other members to borrow the services of any of the employees in their old departments to complete the project.

Case Questions

1. Do you think the consolidation is possible? What possible issues can emerge as a result of consolidation?
2. One of the participants argued about a new system incorporating all the features of old systems. What are benefits of such a system and what problem may rise during the process of development?
3. The organization is undergoing a reorganization that demanded integration of IT systems. Is it possible to run reorganized organization with the old fragmented multi-systems? Why and why not?

13 HARIPURE TELECOM (HT)

The Haripure Telecom (HT) used to use file based databases for its information resources department (IRD) until 2000. The new CEO, Mr. Jaan M. Hoti was originally an IT graduate from London School of Economics and political Science, known as LSE. He examined organizational systems and business process after assuming the headship. He realized that the world was living in 21st century where technology, networks and the internet plays a constructive role in redesign of the work people used to do. Secondly, most of Pakistani public and private organizations are automating their business processes. HT cannot compete with the industry unless it makes changes in its processes and procedures.

Although computer was used for processing business information, but the processes were outdated such as file-based databases. They were not cost effective because of their hierarchical nature, duplication of efforts, poor security etc.

Mr. Jaan held a meeting with key personnel in IT section and members from functional areas. He proposed that a relational database is more effective than a file-based system. He said, "Database system reduces or eliminates repetition, redundancy and inconsistency. Accessibility is made easy; development cost can be achieved". One member of the IT section enquired, how development cost would be reduced when more people will be involved. Mr. Jaan Replied, "Programmers and users can perform ad hoc queries of data in the database1". No other member raised any question that means they offer support for the proposed relational database.

M. Jaan set up a team to redesign database, test and implement it with next six months. He allows development team to replace hardware and supporting software, if necessary, to make the database a reality. Relational database is based on tables or relations. The development team examines existing software, hardware and file-based databases and made a list of the problems associated with the entire infrastructure. They conducted another meeting to decide the structure and number of required tables. The head of IT was sponsor of the project; he distributed the work to members of the team. He monitored the entire development process. A working model of the database was ready after four months of day-in and day-out wok.

The database was implemented in a department first which indicated few problems which were resolved with little effort. The database was rolled out in the entire organization. It works well in the first six months but complaints and queries stated to flow like a flood afterwards. More people were hired to cope with excessive queries and complexities.

The issue was raised in a high-level meeting about the functionality of the database. The head of IT argues that the system worked well during pilot and subsequent roll out phase. Nevertheless, the issues appeared almost abruptly during the sixth month of operation. One of the staff member replied that the problem might emerged due to additional users who started to use the database when the volume of business increased. The hardware and software compatibility or capacity mismatched. There were other suggestions and proposal about the issue, but none of them gave a clue of the problem.

Case Questions

1. What are the possible causes of database functionality?

2. Recall that the CEO allowed, the database development team, to change hardware, if required. But the database was run with "old" machines. Is it a mismatch of hardware/ software?
3. any new system is designed by capturing system requirements. The system developer did not refresh requirements of the user. Do you think it may be one of the causes of the problem? Support your argument with specific examples.
4. If you were the in charge of the database development team, how would you like to develop a similar database? What are the special requirements of a database project than generic software?

14 E-COMMERCE IN VIRTUAL BUSINESS (VB)

The Virtual Business provides basic to advanced technology learning support to small and medium size businesses. B2B involves capacity building, basic IT learning, strategic application of technology, change management and productivity improvement.

Although VB is based in Islamabad yet it operates all over Pakistan because virtual servers are provided through web portals, video conferencing, distance learning and web-based learning. However, a network of representatives is in place to contact prospective individual and business customer in major cities e.g. Karachi, Lahore, Multan, Hyderabad, Quetta, Faisalabad, Sialkot, Sargodha, Peshawar etc. the representatives call on a customer to explain the nature of training and support and explain features of various programs. Customer sign a contract and makes initial payment so that an introduction packs can be posted or an access user name and password can be provided.

A web portal is in pace to provide a point interaction and corroborate the efforts of human network.

The company was set in 2002 by employees of Ufone, Mobilink and Warid as a part time business. However, VB made an Rs.1million profit in its third year of operation. The unprecedented success compels the owner to convert it into a full-time venture. The company was declared a limited company in 2004, three original founders became directors.

A company sectary and five other persons were employed. So, the number of workforce went to nine at the end of the reorganization year. Part-time trainers and experts of various fields are on the payroll, they can be called for support as and when required.

The company is not advertising other than its website and not profiling customer to direct personalize e-mails or special offers. Directors believe that we have enough business; any expansion in the customer-base would reduce quality of what we offer. Rather VB must concentrate on the human network spread in major cities. A new package is under preparation for the representative that propose enhancement of their commission and base rate.

However, customer services have been strengthened through two full time customer service advisors who are responsible to answer any query at extended office hours from 8 am to 10 pm. An auto response system is also in pace which prompt e-mails of customer and informs about the office hours contact numbers.

The turnover is almost steady since 2004 and profit is stagnant at Rs. 1m a year. One of the decline in the VB performance since last three years because the company growth was phenomenal in the first two years. He believes that the company should take appropriate measures to improve sales, number of customers and profit.

Case Questions

1. What should be "appropriate" measures to improve overall performance?
2. : What is wrong (if any) in the company strategy and what can make it good?
3. Since the company is a virtual organization and needs special strategy to concentrate on customer. What that strategy can be? How that strategy will be different from the existing one?
4. A website should be personalized in an attempt to differentiate it from others. How do you personalize your own website?
5. A website is a store front or showroom. Expert say it should be responsive within 12

seconds and customer should receive information after three clicks. Give an example of such a website.

15 KNOWLEDGE MANAGEMENT IN TAASCO

TAASCO was a part of TAACO, a supplier of educational and office furniture company operating in Karachi. When its CEO P. S. Kiyani retired in 2001 who was a resident of central Punjab, he thought to be his own boss. He had ten years' experience in the business and a little money to invest, which he received as a gratuity with a golden handshake from the company. He decided to invest his experience and money in a similar business but in a different geographical region i.e. central Pakistan.

The company was established in late 2001 a similar name TAASCO with a head quarter in Lahore. Mr. Kiyani attended a seminar about management of knowledge during last month of his attachment with TAACO. However, time did allow him to implement the philosophy in TAACO.

He spent few days with colleagues and consultants about how knowledge management may be implemented in his company. Knowledge management involves gathering/ retaining relevant data, turning them into information and knowledge to be used for decision making. Most of the job is done through computers and information technology infrastructure.

He set up an office in Lahore with three rooms: one his own office, the second for his assistant and the third for meeting. His business model was simple but based on modern philosophy. He picked orders through personal contacts; pass on the order to the manufacturer in Chinot with a deadline. He hired an independent expert Quality Control (QC) to check semi-finished (Cora, furniture without polish) and finished products.

A logistics company picks and delivers to the door steps of the buyers. It was also responsible for returns and repairs. QC also monitors the quality of raw materials and related matters.

Mr. Kiyani set up a database to manage and track orders, suppliers and financial matters. The database included order received, its details, customer details and financial receipts and payments because "cash only" was the mode of transaction. Exhibit 1 shows the page of spread sheet designed for the purpose.

This model enables him to analyse each transaction (furniture is a low volume, low transaction business) individually and all transactions collectively on daily, weekly and monthly basis. Manufacturing and distribution cost comprised 40% of the price. A control over them can improve profitability significantly.

Exhibit 1 Components of a spreadsheet
1. Customer code
2. Order size (in units)
3. Monetary value
4. Private/ public
5. Location
6. Order processing time
7. Distribution Cost (which was the logistics co.)
8. Profit from the transaction (give details of each item i.e. purchasing prices, distribution, QC etc.)
9. Customer tracking

Case Questions

1. How Mr. Kiyani can improve his repeat business by using the database information?
2. How the database can be enhanced to improve profitability?

3. Aid Mr. Kiyani correctly to understand the meanings of knowledge management and apply the concept in TASSCO?
4. Which models may be derived from the information contained in the database?
5. If you were the founder and manager of the company, how would you design a knowledge management system for TAASCO? Provide a working model of that knowledge management system.

BIBLIOGRAPHY

Aadamsoo Anne-Mai (2010) Web based project management system, MSc thesis, VaasanAmmattikorkeakoulu University of Applied Sciences

Ahmad Ammar et al, (2007). A review of techniques for risk management in projects, Benchmarking: An International Journal, 14(1), 22-36.

Ajmal, M. and Koskinen, K. (2008). Knowledge Transfer in Project-Based Organizations: An Organizational Culture Perspective. Project Management Journal, 39 (1), 7- 15.

Alshawi, Mustafa and Bingunath Ingirige (2003). Web-enabled project management: an emerging paradigm in construction, Automation in Construction, 12, 349-364.

Altar, S. (2002). Information Systems: Delhi: Pearson Education.

Ambler, Scott W. (2008). IT Project Success Rates Survey Results: August 2007, Accessed 12 August, 2014 from http://www.drdobbs.com.

Andersen, E S, Kristoffer V Grude and Tor Haug (1995). Goal Directed Project Management, Kogan Page, London.

Andersen Erling S. and Anne Live Vaagaasar (2009). Project Management Improvement Efforts—Creating Project Management Value by Uniqueness or Mainstream Thinking? Project Management Journal, 40(1), 19–27.

APM (2013). Accessed 12 August, 2014 from http://www.appliedproductmarketing.com/product_feature_vs_benefit.asp

Awad, Elias M. and Hassan M. Ghaziri (2004). Knowledge Management, New Jersy: Pearson Education Inc., Prentice Hall. Accessed 12 August, 2014 from http://turing.une.edu.au/~comp292/Syllabus/KM_Notes.pdf

Azzopardi, Sandro (2010). The Evolution of Project Management, Accessed 12 August, 2014 from http://www.buzzle.com/articles/evolution-project, Accessed 21 June 2010.

Baker, M.J. 2000. Writing a Research Proposal, The Marketing Review, 1(1), 61-75.

Baldrige National Quality Program (2001). National Institute of Standards and Technology, Accessed 2 August, 2012 from http://www.quality.nist.gov/

Baldry, D. (1998). The evaluation of risk management in public sector capital projects, International Journal of Project Management, 16(1), 35-41.

Barchan, M. (1998). Capturing Knowledge for Business Growth, Knowledge Management Review, 4(September-October), 12-15.

Bond, Unyime E. (2015). Project management, leadership, and performance: a quantitative study of the relationship between project managers' leadership styles, years of experience and critical success factors (csfs) to project success, Doctoral Dissertation, Capella University.

Boyatzis, R. E. & Kolb, D. A., (1995). From learning styles to learning skills: the executive skills profile, Journal of Managerial Psychology, 10(5), 3-17.

Brain, M (Canalys), (2010). Android smart phone shipments grow 886% year-on-year in Q2 2010, Accessed 12 August, 2014 from http://www.canalys.com/pr/2010/r2010081.ht ml

Bruce, D.J. and W.B. Martz Jr. (2007). Information Systems Off shoring: Differing Perspectives of the values Statement. Journal of Computer Information Systems. 47(3), 17-23.

Brue, Greg and Robert Launsby (2003). DESIGN FOR SIX SIGMA, McGraw-Hill Publishing Company: New York.

Cadman, K. (2002). English for Academic Possibilities: the research proposal as contested site in postgraduate genre pedagogy, Journal of English for Academic Purposes, 1(2), 85 –104.

Chuang, M., Donegan, J.J., Ganon, M.W and Wei, K., 2011 "Walmart and Carrefour experiences in China: resolving the structural paradox", Cross Cultural Management: An International Journal, 18 (4), pp.443 - 463

Cleland D.I.Ireland, L.R.(2002). Project management, strategic design and implementation, New York: Mcgraw Hill, p. 35.

Canadian Government (2014). Accessed 12 August, 2014 from http://www.gov.mb.ca/housing/coop/pdf/Phase3Fundamentals_Feasibility_Study.pdf

Carter, C. 2004. Harvesting Knowledge from retirees, KM, Review, 7(4), September/October 2004.

Chuang, M., Donegan, J.J., Ganon, M.W and Wei, K., 2011 "Walmart and Carrefour experiences in China: resolving the structural paradox", Cross Cultural Management: An International Journal, 18 (4), 443 – 463.

Collier D A and James R. Evans (2009) QUALITY MANAGEMENT, South-Western: New York.

Collins, C. and K.G. Smith 2006. Knowledge exchange and combination: the role of human resource practices in the performance of High-technology firms, Academy of Management Journal, 49(3), 544-560.

Conforto, E C and D C Amaral, (2010). Evaluating an agile method for planning and controlling innovative projects, Project Management Journal, 41(2), 73–80.

Cooke-Davies et al, Terence J. (2009). Project Management Systems: Moving Project Management from an Operational to a Strategic Discipline, Project Management Journal, 40(1), 110–123.

Corlien, M. V. et al, (2003). Proposal Development and Fieldwork, Designing and conducting health systems research projects: volume 1, The International Development Research Centre (IDRC), Canada.

Crawford, Lynn H and Lynn H (2009). Government and Governance: The Value of Project Management in the Public Sector, Project Management Journal, 40(1), 73–87.

Cusuman, Michael A and KentaroNobeoka (1990). Strategy, Structure, and Performance in Product Development: Observations from the Auto Industry MIT Sloan School of Management, WP#3150-90 BPS.

Debowski, S. (2006). Knowledge Management, John Wiley and Sons Australia, LTD, 17-18.

Deming, W. Edwards (1986). Out of the Crisis (Massachusetts Institute of Technology, Centre for Advanced Engineering Study, Cambridge, MA 02139, USA).

Donahue, K.B. (2001). Knowledge Management beyond Databases, Harvard Management Update, May 2001, 6-7.

Dosoglu-Guner, B., (2008). Organizational culture as a discriminating variable of export activities: Some preliminary findings, International Journal of Commerce and Management, 17 (4),.270 – 283.

Doyle. S. (2005). Outsourcing woes trouble big companies. Internal Auditor. 62(3), 17-19.

Dutke, S. and T. Rermer (2000). Evaluation of two types of help for Application Software. Journal of Computer Assisted Hearing. 16(4), 307-315.

Ebener, S. et al (2006). Knowledge mapping as a technique to support knowledge translation, Bulletin of the World Health Organization, 84(8), 636-648.

Epa (2014). Accessed 12 August from http://www.epa.gov/agstar/documents/conf12/08a_Ries.pdf

Evaristo , R. and P C van Fenema (1999). A typology of project management: emergence and evolution of new forms, International Journal of Project Management 17(5), 275 – 28.

Ferns, D C (1991). Developments in programme management International Journal of Project Management, 9(3), 148-156.

Fish, K.E. and J. Seydel. (2006). Where IT outsourcing is and where it is going. A study across functions and department size. Journal of Computer Information Systems. 46(3), 96-103.

Francesca, C.M. et al. (2007). Visual Interaction Systems for End-user Development. A Model-based design Methodology. IEEE Transactions on Systems, Man and Cybernetics: part A. 37(6), 1029-46.

Franke, A. (1987). Risk analysis in project management, Project Management, 5(1), 29-34.

Frenzel, C.W. and J.C. Frenzel (2004). Management of Information Technology. Boston: Course Technology.

Friedmann, C. (2004). Knowledge from the workforce, KM Review, 7(4), 2.

Ganssle, Jack. (2008). A million lines of code, Accessed 12 August, 2014 from http://www.embedded.com/design/205604461

Garvin, D., A. (1978). Competing on the Eight Dimensions of Quality. Harvard Business Review, 65, 421-422.

Ghauri, P. et al (1995). Research methods in business studies, London: Prentice Hall.

Gilmour, D. (2003). How to fix knowledge Management, Harvard Business Review, October, 16-17.

Glass, N. (1995). Management Masterclass, London: Nicholas Brealey Publishing.

Golob, K. Majda Bastič; and Igor Pšunder (2013). Influence of Project and Marketing Management on Delays, Penalties, and Project Quality in Slovene Organizations in the Construction Industry, Journal of Management in Engineering, 29, (4), 495-502.

Goraga, M. R. (2008). PAK IT team in Ottawa to enhance trade ties, Business Recorder, 23 April, 5.

Grant, R M (1996). Towards a knowledge-based theory of the firm, Strategic Management Journals, 17, Winter special issue, 109-122.

Greg, H. (2005). Essential elements for managing any successful project, QUE Publishing, Available at: www.Quepublishing.com, Accessed 10 June 2010.

Greg, H. (2008). Absolute Beginner's Guide to Project Management, Rough Cuts, 2nd Edition, QUE Publishing, Available at: www.Quepublishing.com, Accessed 10 June 2010.

Hofstrand, D. & Holf-Clause, M. (2009). What is feasibility study? Accessed 12 August from:

www.exension.iastate.edu/agdm

Hameri, Ari-Pekka (1997). Project management in a long-term and global one-of-a-kind project,

International Journal of Project Management 15(3), 151-157.

Hartman, F and Greg Skulmoski (1999). Quest for Team competence, International Journal of Project Management, 5(1), 10 – 15.

Haughty, Duncan 2010. A Brief History of Project Management, available at: http://www.projectsmart.co.uk/brief-history-of-project, Accessed 17 June 2010.

Hoffer, J.A. et al. 1999. Modern Systems Analysis and Design. New York: Addison Wesley Inc.

Hoffer, J.A., J.F. George, and J.S. Valacich. 2005. Modern Systems Analysis and Design, (4th ed.), Upper Saddle River, NJ: Prentice Hall.

Hofstede, G., 2005 "Cultures & Organisations", 2nd edition, New York: McGraw Hill Publications.

House, R S 1988. The clean Side of Project Management, Addison-Wesley, USA.

Hsu, C. and H.C.Wu. 2006. The Evaluation of the Information Systems: A survey of Large Enterprises. International Journal of Management. 23(4), 817-30.

Hydrocarbon Processing, 2002. Hp Innovations, October Issue, 30.

Iqbal, Javed (2007). Learning from a Doctoral Research Project: Structure and Content of a Research Proposal, The Electronic Journal of

Business Research Methods, 5(1), 1 - 20, available online at www.ejbrm.com.

ISO (2013). Accessed 12 August from: http://www.iso.org/iso/iso_9000

Jaafari, Ali (2001). Management of risks, uncertainties, and opportunities on projects: time for a fundamental shift, International Journal of Project Management, 19(2), 89–101.

Johns, Thomas G (1995). Managing the behavior of people working in teams Applying the project-management method, International Journal of Project Management, 13(1), 33-38.

Juran, J M, (1989). Juran on Leadership for Quality: An Executive Handbook Free Press, New York, NY.

Juran, Joseph and A. Blanton Godfrey (1999). Juran's Quality Handbook, New York: McGraw Hill.

King, A.W. and A L Ranft (2000). Capturing Knowledge: what managers can learn from the thoracic surgery? Board certification process, Academy of Management proceedings MOC, C1-C5.

Klastorin Ted and Gary Mitchell (2013). Optimal project planning under the threat of a disruptive event, IIE Transactions, 45, 68–80.

Korda, A.P., and Snoj, B. (2010). Development, Validity and Reliability of Perceived Service Quality in Retail Banking and its Relationship with Perceived Value and Customer Satisfaction. Managing Global Transitions, 8(2), 187-205.

Kotler, P. 2002. Marketing Management, London: Pearson Education.

Kuklan, H (1993). Effective Project Management: an expanded network approach, Journal of Systems Management, 44(3), 12-17.

Kulon, J.P. Broom head, and D.J. Myanors (2006). Applying Knowledge-based engineering to traditional manufacturing design, International Journal of Advanced Manufacturing Technology, 30, 945-951.

Kumar, P.P. (2005). Effective use of Gantt chart for managing large scale projects, Cost Engineering, 47(7), 14-21.

LaBrosse, M. (2008). 10 Ways to inspire your Team, Available at: www.project Smart.co.uk, Accessed 11 October, 2010.

Laudon K C and Laudon J P. (2006). Management Information Systems. New Jersey: Pearson Education, 416.

Longman Dictionary of contemporary English 1995. Essex: Longman, 786.

Mack, R; Y. Ravin and R.J. Byrd, (2001). Knowledge Portals and the emerging digital knowledge workplace, IBM Systems Journal, 40(4), 925-955.

Manthey, A 2006. Capturing Learning: a learning legacy, Leadership, 35(4), 11.

Mariosalexandrou, (2010), Project Manager Job Description, Accessed 12 August from, http://www.mariosalexandrou.com/free-job-descriptions/project-manager.asp

Maylor,H. (2001). Beyond the Gantt chart Project management moving on. European Management, Journal, 19(1), 92–100.

McManus, J (2014). A project management perspective of information system development, Management Services, Spring, 30-36.

McManus, J. & T. Wood-Harper. 2003. Information Systems Project Management. DEHLI: Pearson Education Ltd.

Merchant, K. A. (1985). Control in business organizations, Marshfiled, MA: Pitman

Meredith, J. and S J Mantel (2010). Project Management: A Managerial Approach, Singapore, John Wiley & Sons.

Milunovic, S and J. Filipovic (2013). Methodology for quality management of projects in manufacturing industries, Total Quality Management, 24 (1), 91–107.

MindTools (2013). Accessed 16 August, 2104 from http://www.mindtools.com/pages/article/ctq-trees.htm

Morris, P (2013). Reconstructing Project Management Reprised: A Knowledge

Perspective, Project Management Journal, 44(5), 6–23.

Murphy, A and Ann Ledwith, (2007). Project management tools and techniques in high-technology SMEs, Management Research News, 30(2), 153 – 166.

Nagaraj, Srinivasan, M Ramachandra and J Ratna Kumar (2010) Cyclic Approach to Web Based Project Management, International Journal of Computer Applications,8(5), 26-30.

Nicholas, J M (2001). Project Management for Business and technology, principles and practices, New Dehli: Prentice-Hall of India Pvt. Ltd.

Nikander, I.O. and Eero Eloranta (2001). Project management by early warnings, International Journal of Project Management 19(7), 385-399.

Nissen, M.E; M.N. Kamel and K.G. Sengupta, (2000). A framework for integrating knowledge process and system design, Information Strategy: The Executive's Journal, 16(4), 17-32.

O'brien, J A. 2002. Management Information Systems, Boston: McGraw-Hill Irwin.

Omar, A. (2009). Uncertainty in Project Scheduling— Its Use in PERT/CPM Conventional Techniques, Cost Engineering, 51(7), 30-34.

Orlikowski, W.J. 1993. CASE tools as organizational change: investigating incremental and radical changes in systems development. MIS Quarterly. 17(3), 309-340.

Oz, Effy. 2002. Management Information Systems. Boston: Course Technology, 490.

Pelc, K.I. 2002. Knowledge mapping: the consolidation of the knowledge management Discipline, Knowledge, Technology, and Policy, 15 (3), 36-44.

Perry, J G. (1986). Risk management - an approach for project managers, International Journal of Project Management, 4(4), 211-221.

Project management institute (2000). A Guide to the Project Management Body of Knowledge (PMBOK Guide).

PROJECT MANAGEMENT INSTITUTE (2004). A guide to the Project Management Body of Knowledge, 3rd ed. Newton Square, PA: Project Management Institute.

PROJECT MANAGEMENT INSTITUTE (2010). Project institution documents, Accessed 12 August from: www.mindtool.com

PulacchiniItaly, Donato (2012). Feasibility studies Methodologies and practices, Turkey Bilateral Cooperation Project.

Raiden, A. B., Dainty, A. R. J. and Neale, R.H. (2004). Current Barriers and Possible Solutions to Effective Project Team Formation and Deployment within a Large Construction

Organization, International Journal of Project Management, 22(4), 309–316.

Rasid, Siti Zaleha Abdul, Wan Khairuzzaman Wan Ismail, Nor Hazlin Mohammad, and Choi Sang Long (2014). Assessing Adoption of Project Management Knowledge Areas and Maturity Level: Case Study of a Public Agency in Malaysia, Journal of Management in Engineering, 30 (2), 264-271.

Reilly, Michael D., Ph. D., Millikin, Norman L., Ph. D. (1996). Starting a Small Business: The Feasibility Analysis. Bozeman, Montana: The College of Business at Montana State University - Bozeman.

Reiss, G. 1995. Project Management Demystified, New York: Taylor & Francis.

Rob, M.A. (2006). Dilemma between the structured and object-oriented approaches to systems analysis and design, Journal of computer information systems, 46 (3), 32-41.

Roberts, G (2005). Groupware as Knowledge Repository, Computers in Libraries, 25 (4), 25-31.

Romney, M.B. and P.J. Stembort. (2003). Accounting Information Systems. DEHLI: Pearson Education LTD.

Rowland-Jones, R (2013). Total Quality Management – TQM, Accessed 10 August, 2014 from www.bsieducation.org/standardsinactipon

Rozenez, S. et al (2004). MPCS: Multidimensional Project Control Systems, International Journal of Project Management, 22(2), 109 – 118.

RUSU, Lucia and Vasile RUSU (2010) Online Project Management for Dynamic e-Collaboration, Informatica Economică, 14(1), 182-190.

Saladis, Frank P. (2003). Taming the Wild Project -- Control Techniques for Project Success, Accessed 12 August, 2014 from http://www.allpm.com/modules.php?op=modl oad&name=News&file=article&sid=653, Accessed 10 June 2010.

Shang, S. and P.B. Seddon (2002). Assessing and Managing the Benefits of Enterprise Systems: The Business Manager's Perspective. Information System Journal. 12(4), 271-99.

Skibniewski, Miroslaw and Gustavo Vecino (2012). Web-Based Project Management Framework for Dredging Projects, Journal of Management in Engineering, 28(2), 127–139.

Small, C. T and A. P. Sage, (2005/2006). Knowledge Management and Knowledge Sharing, Information Knowledge Systems Management, 5, 153-169.

Smith, M. (2007). Fundamentals of Management, London: The McGraw Hill Companies.

Soderlund, J. (2004). Building Theories of Project management: past research, questions for the future, International Journal of Project Management, 22(2), 183 – 191.

Srivastava, A and K.M. Bartol (2004). Empowering Leadership in management teams: effects on knowledge sharing, efficiency and performance, Academy of Management Journal, 49 (6), 1239-1251.

Swanson, E.B. and Danes Enrique. (2000). System Life Expectancy and the Maintenance Efforts: Exploring their Equilibrium, MIS Quarterly, 24 (2), 277-97.

Talbert, N. (2002). Getting the most from an Enterprise System. MIT Sloan Management Review. 44 (1), 11.

Teller, J. (2013). Portfolio Risk Management and Its Contribution to Project Portfolio Success: An Investigation of Organization, Process, and Culture, Project Management Journal, 44 (2), 36–51.

The Feasibility Analysis (2013). Accessed 12 August, 2014 from http://msuextension.org/publications/Business andCommunities/MT199510HR.pdf

Thomas, J L and Mark Mullaly (2009). Explorations of Value: Perspectives of the Value of Project Management, Project Management Journal, 40(1), 2–3.

Thomas, J. & Mullaly, M. (2007). Understanding the value of project management: First steps on an inter- national investigation in search of value, Project Management Journal, 38(3), 74–89.

Tudhope, D, P. Beymon-Davies and Mackay, H. (2000). Prototyping Praxis: Constructing Computer Systems and Building Belief, Human-Computer Interaction. 15, 353-83.

UK Association of Project Management (APM), Body of Knowledge (BoK) Revised January 1995 (version 2), Accessed 13 August, 2014 from www.apm.org.uk, Accessed 21 June 2010.

Vail. III, E.F. (1999). Knowledge Mapping: Getting started with knowledge management, Information Systems Management, 16(4), 16-23.

Valacich, J.S., J.M. George, and J.A. Hoffer. (2004). Essentials of Systems Analysis and Design, (2nd edition), Upper Saddle River, NJ: Prentice Hall.

Verweij, Stefan, Erik-hans Klijn, Jurian Edelenbos and Arwin Van Buuren (2013) What makes governance networks work? A fuzzy set qualitative comparative analysis of 14 dutch spatial planning projects, Public Administration 91(4), 1035–1055.

Vordaweb, (2010). Accessed 12 August from www.vordweb.co.uk.

Wadhwa, A and S. Kotha (2006). Knowledge Creation through external returning: evidence from telecommunication equipment manufacturing, Academy of Management Journal, 49 (4), 819-835.

Ward, Stephen C and Chris B Chapman, (1995). Risk-management perspective on the project lifecycle, International Journal of Project Management, 13(3), 145-149.

Ward, V. (1998). Mapping Meta Knowledge, Knowledge Management Review, 4(5), 10-15.

Wellman, J. (2007). Leadership Behaviors in Matrix Environments, Project Management Journal, 38(2), 62-74.

Wetherbe, J.C. (1991). Executive Information Requirements. Getting it right, MIS Quarterly, 15 (1), 51-65.

White, D and J. Fortune (2002). Current Practices in Projects management – en empirical study, International Journal of Project Management, 20(5), 1 – 11.

Williams, B. K. and S.C. Sawyer (2005). Using Information Technology, New York: McGraw Hill Technology Education.

Wilson, J M (2003). Gantt charts: a centenary appreciation, European Journal of Operational research, 149(2), 430-437.

Yin, R K (2003) Case Study Research: Design and Methods, Thousand Oaks: SAGE.

Zhai Li et al, (2009). Understanding the Value of Project Management from a Stakeholder's Perspective: Case Study of Mega-Project Management, Project Management Journal, 40(1), 99–109.

Zwikael, O, Kazuo Shimizu and Shlomo Globerson (2005). Cultural differences in project management capabilities: A field study, International Journal of Project Management, 23(6), 454 – 462.

INDEX

A

Abacus Browsers Limited ....Xv, 25

AblXv, 25, 27, 28, 30, 31, 33, 34, 36, 38, 40, 41, 44, 48, 49, 50, 52, 53, 54

Activity Chart..40

Allah .... Vii, Ix

Ambler...143

Andersen...143, 144

Azzopardi 144

B

Bibliography 143

Boyatzis...145

C

Central Asian Airways 111

Ceo 113

Cheetham Meat And Poultry.. 5

Cmp.. 5, 8, 9, 10, 11, 13, 14, 17, 23, 24

Competencies 19

Cooke-Davies Et Al..147

Cpm...Xiv, 5

E

Electronic Payment 125

Energile 105

G

Gold 171

H

Haripure Telecom 129

I

Information .... *Xvii, 105, 115, 118, 143*

Information System *108, 118*

Iqra 171

L

Learning *145*

M

Marketing 171

Merchan 34

Merchant 43

Milestones 11, 12, 14, 19

Mobilink *134*

Muhammad ....Vii, 173, 174

N

Ncl 97

Northern Rocks *125*

P

Perry 50

Personnel 7, 9, 10, 11, 19

Professional Books Limited 119

Project 5, 8, 9, 10, 11, 13, 16, 17, 18, 19, 21, 22, 23, 24, 143, 144

Project Control 16, 17

Project Organization 13

Project Planning 8

Projects

   Evaluation.. 5, 17, 147

Prophet..Vii

Ptcl..101, 102, 103

Q

Quality 138

Quran Vii

R

Refaan 105

Review (Case) Questions 24

S

Sharp 28, 30, 34, 38

Software Development 25

Software Development Eagles.. 55

Speed Property Ltd 56

T

Taasco..137, 140

U

Ummah..Vii

V

Vaagaasar.. 144

Virtual Business 133

Vordweb... 27

W

Ward And Chapman..30, 31, 44, 48

The End

ABOUT THE AUTHOR

Dr. Javed Iqbal was born on 16 April 1959 in Rawalakot district Poonch Azad Kashmir. He received his early education from Pilot High School Rawalakot and received his matriculation in 1975 and intermediate from Hussain Shaheed Degree College of the same town. He earned BBA with a gold medal and an MBA with a gold medal from Azad Jammu and Kashmir University in 1986. He was appointed as a lecturer in Business Administration in the same university. Later on, he was selected by the government of Pakistan for higher studies and deputed to the United Kingdom. He received MBA from the University of Hull and PhD from the University of Salford. Dr Iqbal has been working in England in various capacities: professor, director of studies, marketing advisor and academic advisor. Dr Iqbal returned to Home in 2006 and joined Iqra University Islamabad campus as an associate professor. He became the head of department of technology Management in International Islamic University Islamabad (IIUI). He went back to England for some time and re-joined IIUI in 2012. He joined AKU (AJ&K) as professor and Dean Faculty of Management Sciences in March 2015.

He is a distinguished teacher and world known scholar. His article title "Learning from a Doctoral Research Project: Structure and Content of a Research Proposal" has been classed by one of the professors as the best piece of knowledge for doctoral students of Deakin University in Australia.

This paper is widely used and referred all over the world. Dr Javed Iqbal has been nominated by an international organization for the Award of Distinguished Scientist for his research contribution this year. His books on various subjects are available on www.amazon.com. He poetry is to be published soon as well.

OTHER BOOKS BY THE AUTHOR (S)

1. Iqbal, Javed Saani (2017) Virtues of Sickness: Selected Ahadith, available on amazon (Paperback edition)
2. Iqbal, Javed Saani (2017) Prophet Muhammad (ﷺ) as a planning expert, available on amazon (Paperback edition)
3. Iqbal, Javed Saani (2017) Muhammad (ﷺ): His Trials & Tribulations
4. Iqbal, Javed Saani (2017) Sales and Marketing: Selected Ahadith, available on amazon.co.uk. (Paperback edition)
5. Iqbal, Javed Saani (2016) Research Proposals: Contents & Exemplars, available on amazon.co.uk. (Paperback edition)
6. Iqbal, Javed Saani (2016) Responsibilities of Managers: Selected Ahadith, available on amazon.co.uk. (Paperback edition)
7. Iqbal, Javed Saani (2016) Experience: The Journey of My Life, available on amazon.co.uk. (Paperback edition)
8. Iqbal, Javed Saani (2015) Managing Projects, available on amazon.co.uk. (Paperback edition)
9. Iqbal, Javed Saani Understanding Information Systems (2012), Manchester: GRaASS.
10. Digital Divide in South Asia (2011) by Dr. Javed Iqbal, PhD; ISBN: 9789699578120; available on amazon.co.uk. (Paperback edition) ASIN: B005H1OG1Q (Kindle edition)
11. Managing Risk in Projects (2011) by Dr. Javed Iqbal, PhD and Muhammad Rafi Khattak; ISBN: 9789699578090; available on amazon.co.uk. (Paperback edition)

12.Understanding Project Management (2011) by Dr. Javed Iqbal, PhD and Muhammad Nadeem Khan; ISBN: 978969957845; available on amazon.co.uk. ASIN: B005O0JW6Y (Kindle edition)

13.Information Systems for Managers (2011) by Dr. Javed Iqbal, PhD; available on amazon.co.uk. ASIN: B005YAEMPU (Kindle edition)

14.Managing strategic change: a real-world case study (2010) by Javed Iqbal, PhD; ISBN: 978-3838330952, available on amazon.co.uk. (Paperback edition)

175

www.ingramcontent.com/pod-product-compliance
Lightning Source LLC
Chambersburg PA
CBHW071300220526
45468CB00001B/218